THE AMERICAN CONSERVATIVE UNION PRESENTS

AL GORE

AMERICA IN THE BALANCE

KERRI HOUSTON AND PATRICIA FAVA

American Conservative Union
Alexandria, Virginia

Books are available at special discounts for bulk purchases, for sales promotions, premiums, fund raising or educational use. Special condensed or excerpted paperback editions can also be created to customer specifications.

To order by mail please write The American Conservative Union, c/o Mail Marketing, 722 Columbus Street, P.O. Box 738, Ottawa, Illinois 61350. See coupon on last page.

For information: The American Conservative Union
                      www.conservative.org
                      1007 Cameron Street
                      Alexandria, VA 22314

Toll-free Mail Orders: 800-426-1357 (fulfillment office only)
Fax: 815-434-7907
Email: 72557.3635@compuserve.com

Printed in the United States of America.

8   7   6   5   4   3   2   1   /   02   01   00

Contents

Foreword

What is one to make of Al Gore?

The man has spent a lifetime preparing for the presidency. The son of a U.S. Senator, he grew up not in his native Tennessee, but in Washington, DC. Educated in America's finest private schools and colleges, he joined the army during the Vietnam War not in response to his country's call, but because he felt it would dress up his résumé for the day when he would present himself to the voters of Tennessee and, finally, the nation.

His Senate career might best be described as undistinguished. He was a liberal, but that wasn't always reflected in his voting record as he tailored his views to conform with those of the people of his home state. After all, he'd seen his father's political career end because he forgot from whence he came. Gore the younger wasn't about to meet the same fate even if it meant hedging or changing his position when he moved on to a larger electorate.

His first attempt to do that, however, was a disaster. His run for his party's presidential nomination in 1988 revealed him as stiff, patronizing and, worse, mean.

That would have been it, but for the fact that Bill Clinton liked him and decided that he'd make the perfect running-mate in 1992. The two criss-crossed the country as generational and ideological soul-mates and it worked. They were elected and Al Gore got himself another chance.

Now, eight years later, he's running on his own ... or almost on his own. The Clintons want him to win as part of their legacy and so they'll have a friend in the White House as they embark upon new careers. He enters the race as heir to an economic boom the likes of which Americans have rarely seen and this alone should guarantee his election this fall. Indeed, those who measure such things suggest that he will win because of the economy and other factors that have much to do with atmospherics and little to do with Gore's personality or vision.

They may be right, but thus far he's had a difficult time selling himself to the voting public. His campaign has been lackluster and internally self-destructive. He's tried to reinvent himself and cannot decide whether to run for the presidency on his own or as if he's seeking another four years for the team on which he's served so loyally for eight years. The polls since the beginning of the year have been disappointing and don't seem to be getting any better.

He can't seem to escape the man who elevated him to the Vice Presidency no matter what he does ... in part because he's known not as Al Gore, but as Bill Clinton's Vice President, also because it appears that he was an active player in much of the nefariousness that has come to be associated with Bill Clinton and his cronies. Indeed, as I write this, calls are again being heard that a special prosecutor be appointed to look into the man's apparent inability to tell the truth when questioned by law enforcement officials probing fund raising irregularities in which he's been involved.

It is his apparent willingness to play loose with truth in various situations over many years that millions of Americans now find troubling. It seems that he does it not just when it's in his interest to lie, but also at times when he doesn't have to lie. It's inexplicable, but it continues.

This book brings together much of what has been written and debated about Al Gore. Is he an opportunist or an ideologue? Is he maladroit or just plain mean. Those who've faced him in debate or run against him have seen the dark side of Al Gore and don't much like what they've seen. He's a master of negative campaigning and a devotee of "attack dog" politics.

Like many politicians he seems to subscribe to the old adage that the "end justifies the means." But, he's also a liberal ideologue and appears more than willing to use government to achieve his ends ... to tell people how and where they'll live, how they'll get around. To suggest that he's at heart an ecological extremist may be an understatement.

Whether he'll make it to the presidency will depend on how voters react to the real Al Gore who I hope they will get to know during the next few months. This book should help. ACU's Fava and Houston ask what a Gore presidency might be like by probing his vision and while they don't pretend to know if he will be able to flesh out that vision, wonder what the American people would think if he could.

When one watches Al Gore on the stump and analyzes the poll data, one is reminded of the old story about the World's Greatest Dog Food. This stuff was developed by a great company. It was, I am told, the most nutritious dog food ever developed and was launched with great fanfare. But it didn't sell.

Finally, the development team of nutritionists and marketers met with the board of directors to ponder the problem. After hours of debate, a fellow in the back raised his hand, was recognized by the chairman of the board and said that while all the claims about the product were true, the "dogs don't like it."

The question that to be answered this fall is whether the American people, once they get a load of what Al Gore has in store for them, will like it.

—David Keene, Chairman
THE AMERICAN CONSERVATIVE UNION

Introduction

Al Gore is a child of television. In an earlier age he could never have become a player on the national political scene, much less the nominee of the Democratic Party this fall. We hear a lot about how the TV cameras penetrate the false faces of American politicians and expose them for what they are. This is true—but only when the people behind the cameras are pushing for such an exposure. When they want to cover up the truth, they can make the cameras falsify faces as easily as expose them.

The nation has seen Al Gore on television for more than a decade now—first as a presidential candidate in 1988, next as a vice presidential candidate in 1992, and as Vice President of the United States from 1993 until the present. He can show a pleasing face, a photogenic family, and a bland personality.

For ideological reasons, the networks love him; and that love is revealed in the way they have presented him to the nation—as a middle-aged Eagle Scout, still earning politically correct merit badges. Gore the knight-errant of the environment. Gore the champion of women. Gore the paladin of peace. If the American voters come to see Al Gore as the networks intend, he will become the 43rd President of the United States.

And his election could well mean the end of America as we know it.

Don't underestimate this man by dismissing him as a robotic do-gooder or a harmless bag of wind. He is more ideological than Hillary and more careless with the truth than Bill.

He is the nation's worst nightmare, and he is about to happen to all of us.

We are writing this book in hopes that you will read it, weigh what you've learned, and then help ACU do whatever is possible to help inform your family, neighbors, and friends. The future of America is in the balance.

1

Character Counts—
Or Does It?

Today, most Americans agree that the current President of the United States can't be trusted to tell the truth. So if Al Gore is elected in 2000, will he restore credibility to the White House? Will world leaders—to say nothing of the American people—again be able to take the President at his word?

Incredible as it may seem, Al Gore is a bigger liar than Bill Clinton. Clinton lied mostly about sexual escapades. Gore, it seems, lies about almost everything.

One of the best examples grew out of a reception held in Hacienda Heights, California, in April of 1996. Organized by Chinese operatives John Huang and Maria Hsia, the event was held at a Buddhist monastery, where, according to the *Los Angeles Times*,[1] the monks and nuns—who had taken vows of poverty—ponied up $140,000 for the Democratic National Committee.

Actually, they had done no such thing. Hsia had persuaded them to write personal checks to the Democratic National Committee, then the monastery had illegally reimbursed them. They were "straw donors"—fronting for the monastery, which, as a religious institution, was tax-exempt and therefore forbidden by law to make political contributions.[2]

When the *Los Angeles Times* broke the story in October, 1996, some six months after the event, Gore denied there was any wrongdoing.

When it was obvious that the story was about to break, he said on "Meet the Press": "Number one, we have strictly abided by all of the campaign finance laws. Strictly. There have been no violations.... There have been no violations of law, no violations of the regulations. We've strictly complied with every single one of them.... Well, again, there've been no violations of any law or regulations, and there is nothing that has been done that's wrong."[3]

Untrue. The money that passed through those poverty-bound hands came from rich Chinese-Americans who were evading the $1,000 limit on contributions in order to grease the palms of the President and Vice President.[4]

A little over a week later, the Vice President was invited by National Public Radio to explain himself. At that time, he continued to play the role of Holy Innocent:

> The DNC set up the event, asked me to attend it. *It was not billed as a fund-raiser. It was billed as a community outreach event*, and indeed, no money was offered or collected or raised at that event. But after the fact, contributions were sent in, and they came, evidently,—again, I didn't handle any of this. This is the DNC and they should answer questions about it. [emphasis added][5]

But the controversy persisted.

The *Boston Globe*—a newspaper not known for its conservative Republican leanings—investigated documents surrounding Gore's venture in community outreach and reported the following:

> According to documents examined by the *Globe*, three days before the temple visit, the DNC sent Gore's office a

confidential memorandum making clear the event was a fund-raiser, including instructions for Gore to "inspire political and fund-raising efforts among the Asian Pacific American Community." ...

Minutes before the event, Gore press aide Peggy Wilhide described it as "a fund-raiser" to a *Globe* reporter who was traveling with Gore at the time.[6]

Gore was cornered. He seemed to have no alternative. He did-n't just get caught with his hand in the fortune cookie jar, he had his whole head in it. Surely he would now confess all. Thus, three days later the *Globe* reported:

> Vice President Al Gore acknowledged yesterday that he knew a fund-raiser at a Buddhist temple in California was a "finance-related event," reversing two months of denial in which he said he believed the gathering was for "community outreach."
>
> "He knew it was a finance-related event," Lorraine Voles, Gore's spokeswoman, said in an interview last night. "He knew because we looked at documents in a briefing memo that were finance-related."
>
> Gore himself said for the first time, in a television interview yet to be broadcast, that he was aware it was a "finance-related event," according to the official, who declined to be named.[7]

White House rhetoricians must have thumbed their the-sauruses ragged to come up with the phrase "finance-related event" as euphemism for the far-uglier "fundraiser"—since Gore had previously maintained the event was *not* a "fundraiser." (He also called it "a donor maintenance" event.)

Then Gore himself, in an interview with the *Washington Post*, made a distinction between the two without bothering to explain it:

> In retrospect, whether the event was a fund-raiser or not, it was a mistake for the DNC to hold a finance-related event at a temple, and I take responsibility for my attendance at the event, especially since I was informed that this outreach event [*that* phrase again] was sponsored by the Asian-American Leadership Council of the DNC, and participation in the council required a prior donation.[8]

So while seeming to tell all, he was still in denial. On NBC's "Today Show," while appearing to concede all, he took back most of what Ms. Voles had given away.

> I did not know that it was a fundraiser. But I knew it was a political event and I knew there were finance people that were going to be present, and so that alone should have told me, "This is inappropriate and this is a mistake; don't do this." And I take responsibility for that. It was a mistake.[9]

A "mistake," but not a "fundraiser."

By February the White House was forced to release records that revealed what Gore's office knew about the non-fundraiser. Here is what the *Washington Post* reported on February 15:

> White House aides sidestepped or ignored warnings from the National Security Council (NSC) staff about some contacts the president and vice president had with Asian American fund-raisers now under federal investigation, documents released yesterday show.
>
> Vice President Gore's office was told by an NSC staff official to proceed with "great, great caution" in deciding

whether to attend what Gore's office explicitly described
as a "fund-raising lunch" at a Buddhist temple in Los
Angeles last year

   The White House dispatched Vice President Al Gore to
the 1996 event after deciding the concerns were unfounded.[10]

Even a cursory examination of this sequence reveals a decid-
edly Clintonian pattern to Gore's denials: the outright lie—followed by the partial admission—followed by the Houdini-like
semantic escape.

So what happened to Gore? Nothing. On the other hand,
Huang pled guilty to Conspiracy to Defraud and to Impair and
to Impede the Federal Election Commission.[11] Maria Hsia was
hauled into federal court and convicted for "causing finance officials of Democratic National Committee and Democratic cam-
paigns to file false contribution statements with the Federal
Election Commission."[12]

You have to wonder why Al Gore and the DNC weren't
charged with "causing Maria Hsia to file false contribution statements with the FEC." But, as we'll soon see, if you're Al Gore,
you can violate election laws unto perpetuity and never give
them a second thought.

When new employees enter the federal government, they're
immediately and invariably told: You may not use your office
for partisan political purposes. Above all, you can't solicit campaign funds over your government telephone.

Such activities are forbidden under federal law.

But by this time, Al Gore knew the law didn't apply to him.
Not only did he *know* it, he *said* it. And it looks as if he was right!

It all began in 1996, during the Clinton/Gore reelection campaign, when the Democrats were short on cash. Someone had

to get on the phone and call the fat cats. A memo prepared by
Gore's aides for use at a White House fundraising meeting had
him saying this: "So we can raise the money—BUT ONLY IF the
President and I actually do the events, the calls, the coffees, etc."[13]

The moment Gore made the first call, he violated federal law.

When the story of these calls broke, Gore called a press conference and once again claimed he had done nothing illegal. This
time he had a new way of phrasing his denial:

> My counsel—and Charles Burson [sic] is my counsel
> here—my counsel advised me that there is *no controlling legal
> authority* or case that says that there was any violation of law
> whatsoever in the manner in which I asked people to
> contribute to our re-election campaign.... On a few occasions,
> I made some telephone calls, from my office in the White
> House, using a DNC credit card. I was advised that there
> was nothing wrong with that practice. [emphasis added][14]

(The next day, White House officials admitted that Gore had
not used a credit card from the DNC, that he had used a card
issued by the Clinton/Gore campaign committee.)[15]

Gore thought it was perfectly legal to solicit "soft money" for
the DNC rather than "hard money" specifically designated for
the Clinton/Gore campaign. (Besides, he only did it on "a few
occasions.")

The few occasions became 48 when the White House begrudg-
ingly gave an estimate; and the records, finally released, revealed
the total number as 86. ("Just a few occasions.")[16]

Of course, through the miracle of modern alchemy, some of
the soft money he raised was actually transformed into hard
money and ended up in the Clinton/Gore bank account.

Then a DNC memo surfaced with handwritten notes by Gore's

Deputy Chief of Staff, David Strauss, indicating that on November 21, 1995, Gore attended a meeting at which hard-money contributions and fundraising calls were discussed.[17]

On August 8, 1998, the FBI interviewed the Vice President about that meeting and about the memo. In the FBI notes, reproduced below, note the Vice President's forgetfulness, which borders on the pathological.

- "Although Vice President Gore could not specifically recall what was said or discussed at this meeting, he did recall that the DNC budget was discussed, along with activities relating to commercials and the direct mail campaign."
- "He reiterated that he does not have a specific recollection of anything talked about at that meeting."
- "He stated he did not recall anyone saying, or any discussion regarding 65% soft/35% hard. He also did not recall anything being said about hard/soft money relating to the media fund, or about the media fund having a hard component."
- "He did not specifically recall the quote, seemingly attributed to him, 'is it possible to do reallocation for me to take more of the events and the calls?' He offered that although he could not recall this quote at this meeting, it sounds like the kind of thing he would have said, and he probably did say it."
- "The Vice President concluded by saying that Strauss is a truthful and diligent person. If he took those notes at the 11/21/95 meeting, the Vice President would not dispute that what was reflected in the notes was said at the meeting. Vice President Gore simply did not hear those things said."

Why not? Did he have wax in his ears? His own explanation to the FBI interviewers wins the 1998 Slick Willie Prize for Creative Excuses: "The Vice President also observed that he drank a lot of iced tea during meetings, which could have necessitated a restroom break."

Just when it seemed that he might be in real trouble, Janet Reno came through for him, as she has for so many members of the Clinton/Gore Administration. She took the matter under advisement, wrestled with her conscience, and decided the evidence was insufficient to warrant further action.[18]

The *New York Times* would later report that Louis Freeh, director of the FBI, had favored the appointment of an independent counsel. So had Charles LaBella, head of the Justice Department's campaign finance task force, who told Reno in a memo "... the vice president may have given false statements...." (He was soon gone.) Robert Litt, a political deputy, also advised the appointment of an independent counsel.[19]

On Capitol Hill, the Republicans went ape—but to no avail.

A White House spokesman said the President "believes the Vice President has always acted within the letter and spirit of the law."

True in terms of illegal acts he may have committed. However, he's been caught in a number of unprosecuted lies over the past years—so many that it's hard to keep track of them.

Perhaps the most painful distortion of truth was his use of his sister's death to gain sympathy for himself and support for the anti-tobacco campaign—a gut issue for Democrats in 1996. Speaking before the National Democratic Convention, he told the delegates:

> When I was a child, my family was attacked by an invisible force that was then considered harmless. My sister Nancy was older than me. There were only the two of us, and I loved her more than life itself. She started

smoking when she was 13 years old. The connection between smoking and lung cancer had not yet been established. But years later, the cigarettes had taken their toll. It hurt badly to watch her savaged by that terrible disease. Her husband Frank and all of us who loved her so much tried to get her to stop smoking.... Tomorrow morning, another 13-year-old girl will start smoking. I love her too. Three thousand young people in America will start smoking tomorrow. One thousand of them will die a death not unlike my sister's. And that is why until I draw my last breath, I will pour my heart and soul into the cause of protecting our children from the dangers of smoking.[20]

Gore's sister, Nancy, died in 1984, still a young woman—and Gore asserted that her death sent him charging into the world to make war on smoking and the tobacco industry. But his statement is more than misleading.

For years thereafter, the Gores—Albert, Sr. and Al—were still making money growing tobacco on the family farm.[21] In fact, between 1979 through 1990, Gore accepted thousands of dollars in contributions from tobacco political action committees.[22]

According to *Newsday*, during his 1988 presidential campaign, Gore made an almost hysterical pitch to tobacco farmers in which he said:

Throughout most of my life, I raised tobacco," the Tennessee senator hollered. "I want you to know that with my own hands, all of my life, I put in the plant beds and transferred it. I've shredded it. I've hoed it, I've dug in it,

I've sprayed it, I've chopped it, I've shredded it, spiked it, put it in the barn and stripped it and sold it."[23]

He probably didn't do any of that either; but four years after his sister had died, he was still praising tobacco and stroking tobacco growers.

And here's another one.

On Gore's current website (Gore 2000, 10/14/99), he says of the Nuclear Test Ban Treaty, "I've worked on this one for 20 years because, unless we get this one right, nothing else matters."

In fact, he hadn't worked on this one much at all. In 1988, when his fellow Democrats on Capitol Hill advocated a ban on flight-testing of missiles, Gore said to the *Washington Post:* "They took positions that were wildly out of touch with what mainstream Democratic voters believe.... That's not exaggerated political rhetoric, that is absolutely the case. The very idea of having a complete ban on all flight-testing of missiles when we rely on deterrence for the survival of our civilization...."[24]

In 1987, while campaigning for President in Iowa, Gore told the *Des Moines Register* that as an investigative reporter, he "got a bunch of people indicted and sent to jail."[25]

The story followed him back to Tennessee, like a stray dog. Eventually, to get rid of the dog, Gore said he'd made an honest mistake, that nobody went to jail.

In 1988, again on that ill-fated campaign trip, he told the *Washington Post* that while in Vietnam, "I was shot at ... I spent most of my time in the field."[26]

Since no one called him on that one, he repeated the story in 1999, with some embellishment: "I carried an M-16 ... I pulled my turn on the perimeter at night and walked through the elephant grass, and I was fired upon."[27]

Had he gotten by with the tale a second time, he might have awarded himself the Congressional Medal of Honor.

However, *Newsweek* investigated the story and found out the truth. Alan Leo, a veteran photographer in the press brigade, recalls that when he was serving in Vietnam, he was called in by Brig. Gen. K. B. Cooper, an admirer of Albert, Sr., who asked Leo to make sure Gore was sheltered. "He requested that 'Gore not get into situations that were dangerous,'" Leo recalled. Leo accompanied Gore on those "half dozen or so" trips into the field and described them as cakewalks during which, he said, "I could have worn a tuxedo."[28]

According to the *New York Times*, while campaigning against Bill Bradley in 1999, Gore noted that he had backed a sweeping campaign reform bill sponsored by Senators John McCain, Republican of Arizona, and Russell D. Feingold, Democrat of Wisconsin. "Unlike Senator Bradley, I was a co-sponsor of it," Gore said, "and I feel it's very important to get the influence of special interest money out of politics."[29]

The trouble was, Gore never served with Feingold. He left the Senate in 1992 to become Vice President. Feingold was sworn in in 1993.

And there's more.

He told the story many times about how, while at the Democratic Convention of 1968, he had talked to Charles Bartlett, *Chicago Sun-Times* columnist, who was one of the writers working on Hubert Humphrey's acceptance speech. As he tells it, Gore, very young at the time, told Bartlett how he felt; and, sure enough, when Humphrey spoke, he said the very things that Gore had told Bartlett. As Gore himself put it, "[T]here was no doubt Mr. Bartlett had faithfully conveyed some of the feelings that I had tried to describe."

When questioned about the matter, Bartlett said, "I had nothing to do with Humphrey. I had no contact with Humphrey at all." When the *Washington Post* passed this tidbit along to Gore, he quickly said, in wild retreat, "Faulty memory. Faulty memory."[30]

In speaking of the Earned Income Tax Credit (EITC), he told *U.S. News & World Report* in a 1999 interview: "I was the author of that proposal. I wrote that.... That is something for which I have been the principal proponent for a long time."[31]

EITC became law in 1975. Gore was elected to Congress in 1976.

In a joint appearance on "Meet the Press"—when Bill Bradley was talking about his attempt to get the White House to back campaign finance reform in 1993—he said, "the fact of the matter is that no action took place."

Vice President Gore interrupted him.

VICE PRES. GORE: Because all the Republicans voted against it.

MR. BRADLEY: ... what we need to do ...

VICE PRES. GORE: And they controlled the Senate.

MR. BRADLEY: ... what we—where was the effort made, Al, in 1993?

VICE PRES. GORE: We got every single Democratic Senator to vote for it.[32]

The Republicans didn't gain control of the Senate until 1994. If every Democratic senator had voted for finance reform, it would have passed.

Gore told National Public Radio's Bob Edwards, "I certainly learned a great deal from 3,000 town hall meetings across my home state of Tennessee over a 16-year period [in Congress]."

Let's see, 16 into 3,000 goes 187+ times. There are 365 days in a year. That means that if Gore attended a town meeting in Tennessee at least every other day for 16 years, at the end of that period he would still be short by 144 meetings.

These stories abound, and for a while you shake your head. Inventing the Internet. The inspiration for *Love Story*. The man's a laugh a minute. But then you remember that he's running for President of the United States, and suddenly he isn't so funny.

Either he's lying about these matters for political gain—not just once but repeatedly—or he's delusional. There's a lot of evidence to support either view.

2

Al at Full Moon:
Gore's Crazy Environmentalist Agenda

To Al Gore, environmentalism is more than a political cause. It's a secular religion, an ultimate commitment to a belief that cannot be sustained by reason.

Gore is a major prophet of this new religion, a secular Jeremiah predicting the end of the planet if we don't immediately organize ourselves into a worldwide earth cult and make the salvation of nature the controlling principle of our lives. He says all this in his 1992 book called *Earth in the Balance* that is full of pop science, pop theology, pop history, and pop philosophy.[33]

It would be comforting to ignore Gore's view of environmental catastrophe, to believe it's just a quaint holdover from his youth, like a middle-aged man still playing with electric trains. But we can't dismiss this obsession as something irrelevant to his political life. In 2000, he re-released the book just in time for the fall political campaign, reaffirming his belief in everything he said in the original—including his devotion to the earth goddess Gaia.

He cites "a growing number of archaeologists and archaeo-mythologists" who believe that:

> ... the prevailing ideology of belief in prehistoric Europe and much of the world was based on the worship of a single earth goddess, who was assumed to be the fount of all life and who radiated harmony among all living things.... The last vestige of organized goddess worship was eliminated by Christianity as late as the fifteenth century in Lithuania ... it seems obvious that a better understanding of [goddess worship] could offer us new insights into the nature of the human experience.[34]

And what about contemporary Christians — that is, the orthodox ones? It seems they stand in the way of a New World Order that alone can save us from global suicide.

> On the other hand, politically conservative theologians and clergy have inherited a different agenda, also defined early in this century. The "atheistic communism" against which they have properly inveighed for decades is, for them, only the most extreme manifestation of a statist impulse to divert precious resources—money, time, moral authority, and emotional labor—away from the mission of spiritual redemption and toward an idolatrous alternative:

the search for salvation through a grand reordering of the material world. As a result, they are deeply suspicious of any effort to focus their moral attention on a crisis in the material world that might require as part of its remedy a new exercise of something resembling moral authority by the state. And the prospect of coordinated action by governments all over the world understandably heightens their fears and suspicions.[35]

Borrowing a phrase from clinical psychology, Gore theorizes that modern, capitalist society is one big, "dysfunctional family" and that Americans (Americans other than *his* kind of environmentalists) are "addicted" to consumption.

> Industrial civilization's great engines of distraction still seduce us with a promise of fulfillment. Our new power to work our will upon the world can bring with it a sudden rush of exhilaration, not unlike the momentary "rush" experienced by drug addicts when a drug injected into their bloodstream triggers changes in the chemistry of the brain.[36]

He goes on to compare our "dysfunctional society" to "Nazi Germany under Hitler, fascist Italy under Mussolini, and Soviet communism under Stalin."[37] He points out that just as these totalitarian regimes began to expand by taking over a weak and relatively defenseless neighboring society,[38] so do we exploit weaker and poorer nations—the old Yankee-imperialist argument.

> It is not merely in the service of analogy that I have referred so often to the struggles against Nazi and communist totalitarianism, because I believe that the

emerging effort to save the environment is a continuation
of these struggles, a crucial new phase of the long battle
for true freedom and human dignity.[39]

So Americans really *are* like Nazis and Communists; and in
order to eliminate this ongoing evil, we now have to go to war
with ourselves.

In holding to these ideas, Gore is blood brother to the
Unabomber, who made exactly the same arguments in his now-
famous diatribe against technological progress. (If you'd like to
see a comparison between the Unabomber's statements and Al
Gore's, go to the Internet and check out <u>Algore-2000.org</u>.)

The major problem of the book lies in Gore's robotic acceptance of a wildly hysterical analysis of the current environment—
the Chicken-Little view, which holds that global warming is an
undisputed fact, that the ozone hole is growing like crazy, and
that pretty soon the polar ice cap will melt and we'll all drown.

In order to prevent the end of the world—which is right
around the corner—Gore believes we must create a world con-
sortium empowered to intrude itself into every life, every kitchen,
and every bedroom in order to save the earth from extinction.

In fact, in a statement that leaves the reader breathless, Gore
says that we need to take "bold and unequivocal action: *we must
make the rescue of the environment the central organizing principle
for civilization.*"[40] [emphasis added]

To gain some immediate sense of what he wants government
to do, consider this passage about automobiles:

> We now know that their cumulative impact on the global
> environment is posing a mortal threat to the security of
> every nation that is more deadly than that of any military
> enemy we are ever again likely to confront.[41]

Never mind missiles in North Korea or Saddam Hussein's secret build-up or the recent Chinese threat to nuke Los Angeles. Fear, instead, the Taurus in your garage.

He continues:

> Though it is technically possible to build high-mileage cars and trucks, we are told that mandating a more rapid transition to more efficient vehicles will cause an unacceptable disruption in the current structure of the automobile industry. Industry officials contend that it is unfair to single out their industry while ignoring others that also contribute to the problem; I agree, but their point only illustrates further the need for a truly global, comprehensive. and strategic approach to the energy problem.[42]

Having just acknowledged the unfairness of what he's about to propose, he proposes it anyway.

> I support new laws to mandate improvements in automobile fleet mileage, but much more is needed. Within the context of the SEI [Strategic Environment Initiative], it ought to be possible to establish a coordinated global program to accomplish the strategic goal of *completely eliminating the internal combustion engine over, say, a twenty-five year period.* [emphasis added][43]

He doesn't say "abolish the automobile" and bring back the horse and buggy. Instead, he counts on scientists—the same people who ushered in industrial capitalism—to come up with some alternative. He gives them 25 years to accomplish the task.

So obsessed is he with the threat of extinction that he weighs human lives against the lives of trees and ponders the question of which ones are more valuable—and to what degree:

The Pacific Yew can be cut down and processed to produce a potent chemical, taxol, which offers some promise of curing certain forms of lung, breast, and ovarian cancer in patients who would otherwise quickly die. It seems an easy choice—sacrifice the tree for a human life—until one learns that three trees must be destroyed for each patient treated....[44]

Implicitly, Gore also weighs the lives of American children against those of Third World children and leaves little doubt as to which ones are less welcome in his world:

Any child born into the huge consumptionist way of life so common in the industrial world will have an impact that is, on average, many times more destructive than that of a child born in the developing world.[45]

To cure these ills, which he attributes in large part to his own countrymen, he issues marching orders to a whole host of governments and peoples worldwide. Here are just a few of the twelve commandments he proclaims:

1. The calculation of GNP should be changed to include environmental costs and benefits.[45]
8. Nations should revise their antitrust laws to encompass environmental harm.[47]
9. Governments should require the incorporation of standards to protect the environment in treaties and international agreements, including trade agreements.[48]
10. Environmental concerns should be integrated into the criteria used by international finance institutions

for the evaluation of all proposed grants of development funds.[49]

12. Governments should develop an international treaty establishing limit on CO_2 emissions by country and a market for the trading of emission rights among countries that need more and countries that have an excess amount.[50]

In reading this partial list of Gore's non-negotiable demands, you have to be struck by the insistence that environmental concerns be brought into areas where such matters have absolutely no relevance. First, we must redefine Gross National Product (now called Gross Domestic Product) to include environmental costs and benefits. That's like saying, let's redefine your bank balance to include all the good deeds and meanness you've done today. (Trying explaining an overdraft to your banker using that argument.)

Redefinition doesn't change hard economic facts. GDP is GDP, the effect of production on environment notwithstanding.

If you think this kind of bookkeeping is an idea whose time will never come, think again. In 1997, Dr. Henry Miller of the Hoover Institution, in describing current government practice, wrote:

> Mr. Gore's ideology has already infiltrated the workings of our government. Since 1994, the Commerce Department's Bureau of Economic Analysis has used its so-called economic-environmental accounting framework to calculate the country's "Green GDP." Just as a conventional accounting ledger includes an entry for depreciation of plant and equipment, the bureau's system attempts to record the "degradation of natural assets." According to

this Orwellian theory of accounting, grants from the World Bank to radical environmental groups could be counted among the bank's income, while the value of electricity from a new dam financed by the organization could be counted among the bank's expenditures.[51]

This linking of totally unrelated ideas is an indication of Gore's thought processes, which skirt the line between sanity and insanity, perhaps even crossing it.

However high-blown his rhetoric and abstract his reasoning, Al Gore is not all talk and no action. Even before the publication of *Earth in the Balance,* he was striving to put his world plan into practice. Three years earlier, he introduced the World Environment Policy Act of 1989. The bill was a blueprint for Big Government to commandeer the global economy in order to avoid an ecological apocalypse.

For example, Title III decreed the "regulation and phase out of anthropogenic emissions that degrade the environment." Roughly translated, "anthropogenic" means "human produced." This Title specifically charged government with the task of going into your house, garage, car, work place, medicine cabinet, and pantry—and disposing of everything environmentalists believe might enlarge the ozone hole.[52]

Title IV specifically addressed the problems posed by the automobile—which, as you will recall, is more dangerous to national security than any potential world power. Gore's plan: to force manufacturers to increase the miles-per-gallon on new cars to a point where you could drive from New York to L.A. on a thimbleful. And if manufacturers failed to meet the standard, as pre-established in the Act, they would be taxed back into the Stone Age.

Title VI directed international lending institutions like the World Bank to tailor their lending policies to environmental concerns. If this sounds benign, consider this "clarification":

> ... while recognizing the normal needs for confidentiality in banking matters, the Congress finds that actions taken by the World Bank and other international financial institutions can so powerfully influence global ecological issues as to *require a modification of normal banking attitudes.* [emphasis added][53]

If that phrase doesn't strike fear into the hearts of ordinary citizens as well as bankers, then we're in trouble. Here Gore argued that the situation was so grave we had to abandon such outmoded concepts as the free market, and turn our lives, our property, and our businesses over to the experts who alone could save us. Even the World Bank would have a little green elf looking over its shoulder, making sure its every move conformed to government-ordained policy.

Title VIII, entitled "Biodiversity," set up more bureaucracies and red tape to prevent "anthropogenic biological extinctions"— that is, to ensure that every type of fly, scorpion, and leech continued to thrive, even if a million human workers lost their jobs in the process.[54]

Title IX, "Replanting and Conserving the World's Forests," stuck its nose into the timber industry, not only in the United States, but also in such foreign countries as Brazil and Japan. Brazil was ordered to protect the Amazon Basin by convening a conference and identifying problems. Japan was told to restrain itself from consuming tropical hardwoods through quotas and consumption taxes.[55]

Fortunately for the nation and the world, Gore's World Environment Policy Act sank without a trace. But he was still full of proposals, all of which required the active intervention of Bigger and Bigger Government, all of which cost billions of dollars.

In his book, he proposed essentially the same initiatives, with a new name and an increased price tag:

> Improbable or not, something like the Marshall Plan— a Global Marshall Plan, if you will—is now urgently needed. The scope and complexity of this plan will far exceed those of the original; what's required now is a plan that combines large-scale, long-term, carefully targeted financial aid to developing nations, massive efforts to design and then transfer to poor nations the new technologies needed for sustained economic progress, a worldwide program to stabilize world population, and binding commitments by the industrial nations to accelerate their own transition to an environmentally responsible pattern of life.[56]

Like the original Marshall Plan, the conglomerate of programs Gore proposed would cost big bucks. How much? Gore wasn't shy to give the price tag:

> Charles Maier points out that the annual U.S. expenditures for the Marshall Plan between 1948 and 1951 were close to 2 percent of our GNP. A similar percentage today would be almost $100 billion a year (compared to our total nonmilitary foreign aid budget of about $15 billion a year).[57]

The figure $100 billion a year equals roughly $1,000 per American household per year in new taxes. Thus far, no one is taking his Biodegradable Marshall Plan too seriously; but the Clinton/Gore Administration has moved more than a few steps down the Yellow Brick Road in an effort to further the environmentalist agenda. As Gore himself reported:

> We have signed the Biodiversity Treaty, we have begun enforcing the requirements to protect endangered species, we've signed the Climate Change Convention and put forward a climate action plan.[58]

When the NAFTA Treaty was in negotiation, Gore backed a provision that gave participating nations the right to punish the United States for failing to adhere to its own environmental statutes.

In April of 1997, Gore wrote a foreword to a State Department document called "Environmental Diplomacy," which said, among other things, that "[t]oday environmental issues are part of the mainstream of American foreign policy." Again, Dr. Henry Miller of the Hoover Institution points out the Gore influence:

> "Environmental Diplomacy" reads like a Greenpeace manifesto and, not coincidentally, like Al Gore's "Earth in the Balance." ... The remedy proposed by Mr. Gore—and now by the State Department—is to redefine the relevant measures of economic activity. The purpose of this is clear: enabling governments to obscure the costs of environmental protection by calling them "benefits" and to force businesses to list wealth-creating activity as societal "costs." But the effects will be profound: Companies around the world will see their regulatory expenses skyrocket and their markets shrink. Consumers will pay inflated prices for fewer products and higher taxes to support bloated bureaucracies.[59]

So Gore's behind-the-scenes influence in the current Administration is enormous, and he is using his power to promote his environmental agenda—which is anti-business, anti-free-market, and ultimately anti-America.

Gore also played a key role in framing the Kyoto Protocol, which the Clinton/Gore Administration signed in the winter of 1998.

The *New York Times* reported that "the Administration, as expected, will not yet submit the Kyoto Protocol for approval by the Senate, where it faces substantial opposition from critics who say the costs to industry would damage the economy."[60]

"Wreck the economy" would be more like it, which is why the Republican-controlled Senate would refuse to ratify this global sell-out. But Gore obviously sees these treaties as a way to tie the hands of American industries and force them to adhere to regulations and prohibitions created by treaty rather than by law. (Treaties are legally binding when ratified by the U.S. Senate.) Thus the Clinton/Gore Administration is slowly but surely enacting provisions of Gore's World Environment Policy Act piecemeal.

If he were to be elected President, he would not only have a bully pulpit to use to terrify the American public, but also probably have a Democratic-controlled Congress to enact his suicidal agenda and a Democratic Senate to ratify more environmental treaties designed to strip the United States of its preeminent industrial wealth and turn us into the planet's largest Third World Country.

3

Hold On to Your Wallet:
Al Gore Loves Taxes

Al Gore grew up in a tax-and-spend household in a tax-and-spend party in a tax-and-spend era.

His father, Senator Albert Gore, Sr., was a liberal Democrat who believed that the federal government could do most things better than private citizens, including spend their money. During those years, Americans got in the habit of handing over a greater and greater share of their pay without questioning the wisdom or justice of such a tax policy. That was the world in which Al Gore grew up—a world in which Big Government was the greatest Good and ever-increasing taxes the second greatest Good.

So it's no wonder that when Al Gore came to Washington to serve in the House and later the Senate, he should regard heavy taxation as the historical prerogative of his party and oppose virtually every tax cut that came to a vote. He probably didn't have to think about the question, so ingrained was the inclination, so automatic was his response.

Here is a list of his votes on taxation, beginning with his first term in Congress. **Keep in mind that $1 billion in federal spending equals roughly $10 per American household. You can multiply each of Gore's billions by 10 to see what his proposals would cost your family:**

- In 1978, he voted against a $16.3 billion cut in individual, corporate, and capital gains taxes. The tax cut passed 362–49![61]
- The same year, he was one of only 37 Democrats to vote against a tax cut. The tax cut passed 337–38.[62]
- In 1981, he voted against Ronald Reagan's proposal to reduce the highest marginal tax rate from a staggering 70 percent to a slightly-less-staggering 50 percent. The proposal passed 282–95.[63]
- In 1988, while seeking his party's presidential nomination, he attacked fellow Democrat Richard Gephardt for supporting what Gore sneeringly called "the Reagan-Gephardt Tax Bill of '81." (Gephardt shot back: "[T]wo thirds of it went to families that earn $50,000 or less … you bet it was fair to cut taxes for average families.")[64]
- In 1988, during the same campaign, Gore unveiled a new tax proposal: "[I]'ve outlined a series of specific new taxes which I'm not proposing as a first resort, but which should be looked to first in the event preferable measures to reduce the deficit do not work." His proposal included additional taxes on Social Security. Small wonder Gore lost his presidential bid. (Democrats don't like tax hikes either, just spending hikes.)[65]
- In 1990, Gore actually proposed to increase the alternative minimum tax rate from 21 percent to 25 percent. (The motion was rejected.)[66]
- In 1991, Gore introduced legislation to hike the tax rate to 46 percent by raising the highest rate to 35 percent, then adding a surtax of 11 percent on incomes above $250,000.[67]
- In 1992, he voted against tax relief for farmers.[68]

In 1993, as Vice President, Al Gore cast the tie-breaking vote that doomed tax relief for middle-class families. After promising such reductions for the middle class during the 1992 campaign, the Clinton/Gore Administration rammed through a Democrat-controlled Congress what Democratic Senator Daniel Moynihan called "the largest tax increase in the history of public finance in the United States or anywhere else in the world."[69] This bill included the following:

- a $115 billion increase in personal income tax,
- a $31 billion increase in gasoline taxes,
- a $25 billion increase in taxes on Social Security benefits, and
- a $29 billion increase in more Medicare payroll taxes.[70]

In fact, according to a study by the Tax Foundation, the Clinton/Gore Administration has raised the taxes of average Americans by 11 percent—from 30.3 percent of family income in 1992 to 33.5 percent in 1999. The study found that the *typical family* now works more than four months to pay its tax bill.[71]

And what about the future?

As Gore has been quoted as saying, "The Zebra can't change its spots." When asked if he would sign a no-new-taxes pledge, Gore refused. "Nobody has a crystal ball."[72]

And who needs a crystal ball? We have his 22-year record and we also have the Clinton/Gore budget for FY 2000, with new programs that Gore presented to the public in order to give him added visibility for the campaign.

The total for all the old programs and new boondoggles—a breath-taking $1.766 trillion—the largest budget ever conceived by the human imagination. Keep in mind the "$1 billion = $10 of your money" rule when doing the arithmetic here: $1.766 trillion equals $17,660 of *your money*, often taken in taxes hidden from your view, unlike your income tax. The amount is so large that it violates the cap set by the Deficit Control Act by nearly

$33 billion in FY 2000 and $116 billion over the next four years. The *New York Times* drolly reported:

> President Clinton released a $1.766 trillion Federal budget blueprint on Monday that proposes billions of dollars in new spending while preaching fiscal conservatism.
>
> Clinton's budget plan asks Congress for substantial new money for scores of domestic programs popular with liberal and middle-class constituencies, from urban housing vouchers to classroom construction.
>
> The health of the American economy and overflowing Federal coffers allow Clinton to indulge in large new "investments" in politically popular labor, education, health care and environmental projects while cloaking himself in fiscal prudence by proposing to use budget surpluses to pay down the Federal debt.[73]

Clinton allowed Gore to announce many of the programs to seek votes from constituencies that would be funded in the new budget. Early in 1999, the Vice President released the names of the beneficiaries and the amounts they would receive—at the rate of one or two a day, in order to milk the budget story.

The 15 or so programs that he personally trumpeted included:

- $1.381 billion over five years for public transportation and environmental projects, including the expansion of federal wilderness lands and urban parks[74]
- an additional $480 million on schools and educational programs serving Hispanic students, including money for bilingual education[75]
- $1.3 billion to fund disability, health, and nutrition benefits for immigrants[76]
- the largest increase in history for Head Start—$607 million[77]

- $31 million to hire 457 police officers in 144 communities over the next three years. (Do the arithmetic on this one.)[78]

If the FY 2000 budget is a bank-breaker, what would President Al Gore propose for FY 2002?

4

What's Good for Me Is Bad for You:
Gore on Education

In a TV ad aired during the primary season, Al Gore claimed to be "the only Democratic candidate to make education a priority." The ad promised a "revolutionary plan to improve education by over 50 percent."

The 30-second spot included no specific details about Gore's plan, but you can be certain it includes feeding billions and billions of dollars to a failed system without really reforming it. Take, for example, his scheme for pre-school education.

He claims it will cost a mere $50 billion, which adds up to $500 for you and your household, not small potatoes. However, Isabel Sawhill of the liberal Brookings Institute took out her calculator and determined that the plan, which would cover all three- and four-year-olds, would actually cost at least $200 billion over 10 years.[79] (When you're talking about education, of course, it's easy to overlook $150 billion.)

But we're already spending more money per capita on education than the vast majority of industrialized nations, and we've been increasing our expenditures at a prodigious rate.

- The U.S. Department of Education reports that a record $324.3 billion was spent on elementary and secondary education for 1997–98—an increase of almost 88 percent over the past decade.[80]
- Per-pupil spending on education has also spiraled—by 187 percent since the 1960s.[81]
- U.S. Department of Education spending is likewise on the rise. Between 1994 and 1999, spending increased 55 percent.[82]

One of the problems with current funding of education is where the money is going. The Clinton/Gore Administration wants to allot a larger and larger portion to the Washington bureaucracy in order to control curriculum, perpetuate the status quo, and stop genuine reform dead in its tracks. Conservative reformers don't mind spending money on education, but they want to see more of it flow freely to parents.

In fact, in October of 1999, the Republican House approved a measure that would allow 95 percent of federal dollars to flow directly to the classroom and not be bottled up in the Washington reservoir.[83] But don't expect President Gore to sign that one more quickly than President Clinton did. Both men live comfortably in the watch pocket of the NEA, the national teachers' union—the single most powerful force in the Democratic party.

The trouble is, the way the system works, we've gotten next to nothing for our money. To the contrary, by virtually every measurable standard except funding, our public school system has fallen into a steep decline. Part of the problem lies in the fact that schools don't have to get better, indeed have no real incentive to get better. Regardless of performance, the money rolls in—from local government, from state government, from federal government.

Disgusted with the public school system, more and more parents are sending their children to private schools or teaching them at home.

Two of those parents are the Gores. Both Al and Tipper attended pricey prep schools. So did all four of the Gore children. As a consequence, they were never exposed to the problems faced by public school children, whose parents couldn't afford the luxury of a private education.

Yet Al Gore, like Bill Clinton (whose daughter also went to private school), opposes vouchers that would give poorer families the option he had—the ability to choose the best school for his children. In fact, in his primary campaign, Gore featured a TV ad entitled "Vouchers" to express his opposition to this idea. In the 30-second spot, Gore said:

> I think it would be a big mistake to drain money away from our public schools with vouchers that give public money to private schools.

In the first place, if you gave vouchers to poor parents, the funds wouldn't be taken from the public schools system. Perhaps the most successful federally funded education program in history was the GI Bill, which a grateful nation created immediately after World War II to educate returning veterans. The program worked as follows:

- The federal government allotted a sum of money to each veteran to use for tuition, books, and other expenses.
- The veteran could choose any institution of higher learning,

public or private, so long as it was certified as a legitimate
institution of higher learning.

- The college or university could maintain its admissions standards and accept or reject a veteran just like any other
applicant.

At the time this program was inaugurated, no politician
objected that public funds would be going to private institutions.
Everyone thought the program was sound and believed those
who benefitted from it were deserving. As a consequence, more
young men and women earned a college degree than at any other
time in history. A whole generation was better educated and
therefore earned higher incomes. The post-war economy
boomed. And the federal treasury reaped a huge reward, because
higher incomes resulted in more affluent taxpayers.

Most proposed voucher systems would work in the same way.

- The government would allot to the parents of each school-age
student a set sum of money to use for tuition, books, and other
expenses.
- Parents could choose from among the available schools, both
public and private.
- Private schools would have the right to maintain their traditional admissions standards and accept only those applicants
who were qualified.

So why would someone like Gore—who loves to throw
money at education and the poor—oppose a program designed
to help families whose children deserve a better education?

The main reason is that the National Education Association,
one of the most powerful unions in the nation, is terrified of
school choice. The union's bosses know that vouchers will intro-

duce into primary and secondary education a new element—
that of competition.

If, by receiving vouchers, parents can decide for themselves
where their children will go to school, then how many would
choose the public school system? In many areas of the country,
very few. This would cripple the NEA's dues income.

And what would this competition force the public schools to
do? Reform. Clean up their act. Compete or go out of existence.
Try something new. Or old.

That's precisely what businesses must do in order to survive—
give the customer something better than the competition. For
the first time in memory, like business, our public school system
would again be accountable and competitive.

And U.S. students would be getting a better education in the
process.

But the National Education Association doesn't really care
about students or their parents. As Sandra Feldman, president
of the American Federation of Teachers, said on "Meet the Press,"
"I represent teachers. That's who I represent."[84] Not the kids.

In fact, the NEA doesn't really represent teachers, at least not
in its major activity—the pursuit of a hard-Left political agenda
the organization trumpets yearly in a series of strident resolu-
tions, only a few of which concern education. A sizable percentage of classroom teachers is embarrassed by these leftist
pronouncements on monetary policy, social issues, and even
international affairs—but in many states, union membership is
mandatory so their dues finance political activity they strongly
disagree with.

Of course, Al Gore isn't embarrassed by the NEA's political
postures, because he shares them; and that's why he put an ad
on TV opposing vouchers—to galvanize the NEA vote.

Ironically Gore and the NEA stoutly profess their support of a "woman's right to choose." They mean, of course, the right to choose abortion. But both oppose a woman's right to choose which school her child will attend.

Both Gore and the NEA are committed to "equal opportunity" in the work place. (Who isn't?) But they hate the very thought of equal opportunity in education.

Al Gore won't even give the idea of school choice a chance. In 1992, when proponents introduced a modest bill authorizing $30 million for six demonstration projects—giving low-income families money to enroll their children in the school of their choice, public or private—Gore voted against it.[85]

This bill, which was rejected by the Democratic Senate, would have given both Democrats and Republicans, conservatives and liberals, answers to their questions about school choice and vouchers, questions such as:

- Will choice and vouchers destroy public education, as Gore and the NEA insist?
- Will choice and vouchers force public schools to improve, as proponents argue?
- Will parents make wise choices when they are empowered to do so?
- Will making private schools the indirect beneficiaries of government funding—as was done in the case of the GI Bill—somehow corrupt private as well as public education?

These questions might have been answered by six small demonstration projects—and without threatening the stability of the educational system as a whole. But Gore and other liberal Democrats wouldn't even give the project a chance, despite the fact that among the sponsors were Senators Joe Lieberman (D-

Conn.) and Bill Bradley (D-N.J.). The proposal was rejected by the Senate.[86]

If Gore really believed school choice and vouchers would have a measurably negative effect on public schools, then why didn't he vote in favor of the demonstration projects and prove to school-choice advocates that they were wrong in their predictions of improvement? Then, he could have ended the debate and moved on to other solutions to educational problems.

Obviously, he wasn't so sure of himself. He may have conjured up visions of a wildly successful experiment resulting in more competitive public schools, greater attention to basics, and improved scores on standardized tests.

Such a result would usher in genuine educational reform—and no one has opposed constructive change more ferociously than the National Education Association. Virtually every new measure proposed by serious reformers has been immediately demonized by the NEA or else neutered to conform to current practice.

On the one hand, the NEA wants to tear down American society and rebuild it along "democratic socialist" lines. On the other hand, the organization wants the public school system to roll on like Old Man River—and we all know that rivers roll downhill.

Yet Gore never misses an opportunity to stroke the NEA. And the NEA returns the favor through enormous campaign contributions and the work of tens of thousands of teachers on election day.

In 1996, at a joint meeting of the NEA and the AFT (American Federation of Teachers), Gore brought cheers from the crowd by attacking school choice for low-income parents. The *Houston Chronicle* reported the speech as follows:

Later, at a joint reception of the National Education Association and the American Federation of Teachers—honoring Education Secretary Richard Riley—Gore expanded his comic routine.

He got a cheer by pledging again to oppose school vouchers, a proposal supported in the Republican Party platform to let public-school students switch to private schools.

"We will not tolerate an assault on the fundamental structure of educational opportunity," Gore said.[87]

Yet "assaulting educational opportunity" was precisely what he was doing at that very instant.

In 1998, again speaking before the NEA, he attacked Milwaukee's school-choice program. It's worth noting that this program was engineered by Polly Williams, a liberal black activist from Milwaukee who was tired of seeing children in her part of town condemned to a miserable, useless education just because their parents couldn't afford private schools. She saw the slow, tentative movement of current reform efforts and wanted to make something happen—fast. So she began speaking out in favor of school choice with vouchers.

Because she was who she was, liberals had to listen; and because vouchers were the best solution to inner-city-school problems, conservative reformers stood behind her as well. The result: the first real voucher program in the nation and an immediate pledge from the local school system to make improvements.

So what did Al Gore say about Polly Williams and her dream for a better-educated generation of black Milwaukeeans?

This movement on the part of some people to try and build more support for vouchers, taking money away from

public schools and shifting them [sic] to private schools, I
think, is a very dangerous development and should be
responded to.... Most of them [voucher programs] are just
fraudulent, in my opinion, and would result in severe harm
for the public school system.[88]

It would be interesting to see how Gore would explain his
position to Polly Williams and the poor low-income children of
Milwaukee who, for the first time in their lives, were given hope
and the chance to live the American dream. Would he order them
to return to drab, ineffectual classrooms because somehow their
attendance at private schools was jeopardizing the survival of
the very schools they left behind? And how would he answer
them if they said, "How do you know what it's like to go to
school in South Milwaukee? You and your wife and your kids
all went to private school. Can't we have the same opportunity?"

Gore continues to talk about his commitment to education,
particularly when he is speaking to the NEA; but neither he nor
this dictatorial teachers' union shows any real interest in improv-
ing a system that is failing our children.

5

The Company He Keeps:
Special Friends and Special Interests

Al Gore has often been depicted by the media as a middle-aged Boy Scout, Mr. Clean, the most straight-laced White House presence since Calvin Coolidge. And for years the American people, in the absence of evidence to the contrary, have accepted this characterization. However, since he entered the 2000 presidential race, investigative journalists have begun to peel off Gore's veneer, to expose the lies he's told, the deals he's cut, the laws he's broken.

Thus far, however, most haven't taken a close look at the company he keeps. Here, then, is the low-down on a few of Al Gore's good friends and political cronies—the leeches and manipulators who have surrounded him since he first ran for office.

Tony Coelho recently resigned as Al Gore's campaign manager. He cited a stomach problem as his reason. However, he may have left because the media snoops were hot on his trail.

Coelho was originally called in after the Gore candidacy had washed up on the beach and lay dying in the noon-day sun. When Tony came to the rescue, he demanded "total control" of the campaign organization—and got it.[89]

A few years earlier, he had been one of the most powerful men in Congress. Then, all of a sudden, he was gone—resigning after questions were raised about his ethical conduct. He quit because they had him nailed. Gone but not forgotten: Two years ago he was appointed U.S. Commissioner General for Expo 98, to be held in Lisbon, Portugal.

It was a low-profile job with a high potential for waste, fraud, and abuse. And sure enough, Tony got into trouble again.

In September of 1999, an audit by the State Department's Inspector General found mismanagement of government funds and possible violations of the law.[90]

Below are some of the items on a lengthy list of the abuses the I.G. uncovered: [91]

- Coelho and friends misused around $150,000 in airline tickets and pass upgrades donated to the federal government by Continental Airlines.
- Coelho scarfed up $800 from the petty cash drawer to pay for a Mercedes with chauffeur, though he had 6 vans assigned for his use.
- He stayed in a luxury apartment that cost $18,000 a month and sent the bill to the United States Information Agency.
- He hired two stepsons of the ambassador to Portugal, one as a "senior operations assistant" to work out of his office and paid them inflated salaries. Their contracts did not outline duties. Coelho's niece was also on the payroll.
- He hired a consultant and paid him more than $26,000 to work out of his office, reimbursing him for expenses that weren't covered in the contract.
- He obstructed the I.G.'s investigation by ordering documents destroyed.
- According to the I.G., he wheedled a $300,000 personal loan from the president of a Lisbon bank, ostensibly to support the Luso-American Wave Foundation, formed to raise money for a massive sculpture to honor Portuguese who immigrated to

the United States. Coelho didn't bother to list the loan on his financial disclosure form. At first, the money was deposited into USIA trust funds for the exposition, but was removed after discovery that it was a personal loan and not a gift.

After the I.G.'s report hit the news, Coelho began to engage in damage control, though his efforts weren't entirely successful.

- On October 2, 1999, Stanley Brand, Coelho's lawyer, said the loan "was paid off with donations from people donating to the memorial, including a large donation from Tony himself."[92]
- Two days later, Brand did a bit of back-pedaling. This time he said that Tony still owed around $100,000 on the loan, and was "in the process of paying it off."[93]
- On October 7, Brand gave the world an update: Coelho had sent a wire transfer to a bank in Portugal for final payment on the loan. Reportedly, Coelho had made almost $2 million during an 18-month period, and his total assets were around $55 million.[94]
- Shortly after the story broke, Al Gore said on "Face the Nation": "Tony Coelho is doing a terrific job. He's my close friend, and he's going to continue to do a great job." When asked about the audit, Gore called it "inside baseball."[95]

That might have been the end of it, but it wasn't. In March of 2000, *Time* reported that Coelho's activities in Lisbon were no longer the sole concern of the State Department. The Justice Department had launched its own criminal investigation.[96]

When asked about these new developments, Gore sounded like a broken record: "Tony Coelho is doing a terrific job, day after day. He will continue to do a terrific job."[97] Gore seemed to be saying, "I don't care if Tony's a bad guy, as long as he keeps my campaign ginning."

Within a week the national press was talking about a new investigation—this one by the Securities and Exchange Commission, involving Thoroughbred Breeders, Inc., a corporation that Tony and an unsavory partner took over and then shut down.

A second company, the AutoLend Group, was also under investigation. These companies had two things in common: (1) They were engaged in shady business practices, and (2) Tony Coelho was a director on both boards.[98]

During this scrutiny, Tony Coelho was still the absolute ruler of Al Gore's presidential campaign; and while the major news magazines and the *New York Times* covered this story in depth, the majority of the American people didn't know Coelho was Gore's campaign manager, much less that he'd been involved in so much sleaze.

Now that Coelho has departed, it looks as if Gore will weather another storm without even having to put up his umbrella.

Meanwhile another friend of Al Gore was covering himself with sleaze. This one agreed to plead guilty in Florida to the charge of soliciting a political donation from a foreign contributor in behalf of the Democratic Party. According to prosecutors, Howard Glicken solicited the contribution from German businessman Thomas Kramer.

The *Wall Street Journal* reported the following:

> The case generated controversy after FEC lawyers recommended against pursuing Mr. Glicken because it was "unclear" that he would settle the case, given his "high profile [and] potential fund-raising involvement in support of" Mr. Gore.

Mr. Gore met Mr. Glicken in 1987 during the then-senator's unsuccessful bid for the presidential nomination and the two became friends. He raised more than $2.3 million during the 1992 and 1996 Clinton/Gore campaigns, and Bill and Hillary Clinton listed him among their "longtime friends" who stayed overnight at the White House. After the 1992 election, Mr. Glicken became a consultant to foreign businessmen and introduced associates to key people in Washington, squiring some to fundraisers to meet the president and other players. He visited the White House more than 70 times.[99]

One of the most fortuitous friendships Al Gore and his family ever made was with Armand Hammer and his Occidental Petroleum Company. Younger Americans aren't familiar with the controversy that surrounded Hammer during his long and contradictory life. One of the richest men in the world, he was an outspoken supporter of the Soviet Union and international communism during the Cold War. Many Americans saw him as a traitor, and J. Edgar Hoover believed that he acted as a Soviet agent while traveling to and from Russia. As Micah Morrison of the *Wall Street Journal* pointed out, citing an authoritative book on the subject by Edward Jay Epstein, Hoover's suspicions were grounded in hard evidence:

Mr. Hammer mined asbestos and brokered the production of tractors and pencils for Stalinist Russia. He cut lucrative fur deals. He trafficked in Czarist art, real and forged. He laundered millions for the Soviet Union in sham transactions. Later, Mr. Epstein reports, Mr. Hammer leapt into the big time by acquiring Libyan oil rights for Occidental Petroleum through a combination of shrewd dealing and bribery.[100]

Hammer also did something else. As Morrison put it, he "trafficked in politicians of all parties and stripes."[101] One of these was Albert Gore, Sr. Another was Albert Gore, Jr.

Hammer and the elder Gore met at a stock auction in the 1940s and established a close friendship that lasted until the 1990s, when both men died.[102] Both were men of the Left, and both were driven to become the rich capitalists they despised in the abstract.

And they both profited enormously from the relationship.

Early in the game, one of Hammer's subsidiary companies bought a piece of property in Tennessee, sold it to Gore, Sr., who in turn sold it to Gore, Jr.—our Al. Hammer's company then began paying Gore, Jr. a highly inflated annual fee for mining rights—*and never mined the property.* This little arrangement netted Gore, Jr. over $190,000.[103]

Hammer did other favors for Gore, Sr. For example, the two men went into the cattle business together. As Morrison put it:

> Over the years, as Mr. Gore rose in prominence and went on to the Senate, many favor-seekers traveled to Tennessee to purchase some very expensive cattle. The profits allowed the senator and his family to live in luxury at Washington's Fairfax Hotel. In return, Mr. Gore provided several valuable services to Mr. Hammer, including fending off the FBI.[104]

Hammer also did favors for Gore, Jr., in addition to paying him mineral rights.

- When Senator Al ran for reelection in 1990, the Hammer family and corporations made donations up to the legal limit.[105]

- According to Neil Lyndon, Hammer's former personal assistant, Al and Tipper had dinner regularly with Hammer and Hammer's paid lobbyists. The *Wall Street Journal* also quotes Lyndon as saying: "Separately and together, the Gores sometimes used Hammer's luxurious private Boeing 727 for journeys and jaunts."[106]

- The *New York Times* reported the following: "Former Senator Paul Simon of Illinois wrote in a 1989 book that Mr. Hammer promised him 'any cabinet spot I wanted' to withdraw from the 1988 Democratic presidential primary race and support the younger Mr. Gore's candidacy."[107] It's particularly interesting that Hammer should feel free to make such an offer. Did that mean Gore was so much his creature that Hammer could make such promises without even consulting the candidate? Or did it mean that he was acting as Gore's agent in the matter?

Why was Hammer so anxious to help further Gore, Jr.'s career? Perhaps events this year provide us with an answer to that question.

Near Bakersfield, California, lies Elk Hills oil field, a 47,000-acre tract that has belonged to the federal government since 1912. In September of 1995, the Vice President of the United States, in his role as Reinventer of Government, recommended that Elk Hills be privatized. When the land was released for sale, Occidental Petroleum gobbled it up. Occidental stock soared. And the trust fund Al Gore's father left behind contained a huge block of stock. Al is currently managing that trust for his mother. It's certainly satisfying to be able to help your country and your gray-haired mother at the same time.[108]

No one knows the extent to which Gores Sr. and Jr. aided

Armand Hammer, his family, and Occidental. Nor can we deter-
mine the extent of the services Hammer rendered to the Gores.
These are relationships common enough in Washington. But Al
Gore has been involved in more than his share.

One of the most sinister figures in Al Gore's entourage is
Nathan Landow—a man with a shady past and even shadier
connections. In the 1970s, Landow made a serious effort to get
into the hotel and casino business. When he was ready to make
his move, he enlisted the help of Joe Nesline—an underworld
character. As the *Washington Post* put it in 1978:

> Two prominent Washington investors with connections
> to the Carter administration were involved in a proposal
> to build a hotel and gambling casino in Atlantic City, with
> Washington gambling king pin Joe Nesline as a consultant.
> The investors are multimillionaire builder Nathan Landow
> and Smith Bagley, a Reynolds tobacco heir. Landow is
> under consideration for appointment as U.S. Ambassador
> to the Netherlands.[109]

The *Post* also pointed out that Nesline had a long criminal
record, including bookmaking, bribery and gambling. In 1951,
he was also convicted of carrying a deadly weapon in the fatal
shooting of a man in an after-hours club.[110]

Landow and Nesline were also involved in another casino
deal, this one on St. Martin Island in the Caribbean. This enter-
prise also involved Edward Cellini, brother of mob associate
Dino Cellini, a former associate of Meyer Lansky.[111]

In yet another business deal, Landow teamed up with
Anthony Plate, a member of the Carlo Gambino crime family,
to invest in Quaker Masonry, Inc., a firm with offices in Maryland
and Florida.[112]

In the early 1980s—when the administration of Washington

mayor Marion Barry was selling urban renewal properties to Democratic Party supporters at cut-rate prices—Landow was one of the lucky buyers. As *National Review* reported: "Nathan Landow, for example, a prominent Democratic Party fundraiser, paid less than one-third the market price for a piece of downtown real estate he purchased from the [Washington Redevelopment Land Agency] in early 1982."[113]

So Landow has been skulking around in deep shade for several decades—and during this period he was a big behind-the-scenes money man in the Democratic Party.

Question: What are Landow's connections with Al Gore and the Clinton/Gore Administration?

Answer: Many and varied.

- Landow raised $600,000 for the Clinton/Gore ticket in 1992 and 1996—a lot of money that buys a lot of gratitude.[114]
- He allegedly tried to pressure former White House volunteer Kathleen Willey to keep quiet about Bill Clinton's sexual harassment. According to *Newsweek*, "Landow's real-estate firm chartered a plane to fly Willey from her home to Maryland's Eastern Shore, where Landow has an estate." There, according to *Newsweek*, Landow told her, "Don't say anything," that if she said "nothing happened," no one could contradict her. Willey told the grand jury that during her visit, "Landow offered to fly her to New York City for a Christmas shopping trip."[115]
- The *Washington Post* reported that Jarrett Stern, a private investigator, said Landow hired him to spy on Willey, According to Stern's lawyer, the P.I. called Willey and warned her. Landow denied he hired Stern.[116] It turned out he was telling the truth. It was Landow's lawyer, Saul Schwartzbach, who hired the investigator to spy on Willey.[117]

- The *Washington Times* reported that when Cheyenne and Arapaho Indians were attempting to get the government to return tribal lands, "Longtime Gore fund-raiser Nathan Landow and former Clinton-Gore campaign manager Peter Knight reportedly offered to lobby the administration for the return of the lands in exchange for campaign contributions from the tribe of more than $100,000. . . . For their efforts the Indians got lunch with President Clinton and a dinner invitation from Mr. Gore, but no land. When news of the shakedown broke earlier this year, the Democratic National Committee returned the money."[118]

- But Landow wasn't merely shaking down poor Indians for the good of the cause. He also tried to grab a piece of the action. As *U.S. News & World Report* put it: "Although officials of the Cheyenne-Arapaho tribes ultimately refused to testify in the case, tribal lawyer Richard Grellner told the Senate Governmental Affairs Committee that in exchange for help with their claim, Landow demanded 10 percent of any development revenues and gas or oil royalties on the disputed land—a bonanza possibly worth as much as $200 million."[119]

- Archie Hoffman, former Cheyenne-Arapaho tribal secretary, when interviewed by Bill Moyers on "Frontline," said of Landow, "And he said, but if we didn't do that, he said he'd make sure we never got the property back, you know?"

- It gets worse. When federal investigators began to look into Landow's dealings with the Cheyenne-Arapahos, Michael C. Copperthite, a Democratic fundraiser, knew some of the detail—and Landow knew that he knew. So according to Copperthite, Landow "did exactly the same thing to me" that Willey said he'd done. Here's Copperthite's version: "He said, And I quote exactly: 'You're going to be contacted by Justice

Department people probably and I want to go over with you what the truth is, so that you can tell the truth.' ... So then he does this whole story that doesn't even match up to anything that happened and then says, 'Now that's the truth, isn't it? You're going to tell the truth.'"[120]

- According to Copperthite, Landow's offer for lying to the Justice Department was not a Christmas shopping spree in New York, but a job with Al Gore's 2000 presidential campaign.[121]
- So where did Nathan Landow get his clout with Gore? It was Landow who came to Gore and urged him to run for President in 1988, so the two go way back. And in that race, Landow was Gore's chief financial backer. According to Copperthite, Landow told him, "We're all going to be part of the big happy Gore family some day and this all will pass over." Copperthite's interpretation: "He was clearly telling me to keep my mouth shut, play along and I would be taken care of—or un-taken care of."[122]

Al Hunt, writing in the *Wall Street Journal*, reported that Landow also apparently joined others in trying to help Webster Hubbell out of his financial difficulties. Then Hunt says something about Landow that's significant:

What sets Mr. Landow apart, however, is that he and Bill Clinton actually have a hostile relationship. But Mr. Landow is close to Vice President Al Gore. Political observers who know him say that it's highly doubtful that Mr. Landow would have done this out of personal kindness rather than political calculation. . . .[123]

It's important to note that all of these characters—slipping in and out of the White House, representing special interests, peddling influence—were invited into the party by Al Gore. Indeed, looking over this abbreviated list, it's easy to conclude that Gore's friends are even sleazier than Clinton's friends, a terrible revelation to a sleaze-weary public.

6

Democrats Trashing Democratic Programs
Say Anything, Get Elected!

Huey Long has been quoted as saying, "If you have the reputation of an early riser, you can sleep until noon."

The Democrats have the reputation of inventing and defending Social Security, Medicare, and Welfare; so they feel they can gouge these systems without answering to the electorate.

The time has come to expose this shell game. Here are some hard facts about the Clinton/Gore Administration, Al Gore, and the Social Security/Medicare/Welfare programs.

First, let's look at Social Security.

Democrats have perennially accused Republicans of trying to take away money from retired people—and many of the elderly, frightened out of their wits, believe the lie. Yet the very reverse is true.

Take, for example, the earnings limit on Social Security benefits. After spending a lifetime paying money into the system, many people eligible to retire on Social Security benefits chose

to remain in the work force. In making this choice, they have to
to continue paying part of their earnings into Social Security.

But, if they earned more than a certain amount they weren't
allowed to draw full benefits from the system, even though they
had paid into the system and reached the age of eligibility.

Republicans thought this was unfair. Why? Because they
tended to regard Social Security as if it were an annuity—an
investment a worker makes over the years in order to reap
retirement benefits at a certain age. When you reach that age,
you start receiving the funds you've invested—plus interest.

Democrats, on the other hand, have tended to see Social Security as a form of welfare—an income that should come only to
those who need it badly. Never mind that a worker may have
paid thousands of dollars more into the system than he or she
can ever collect. If the worker earns more than a certain amount—
no benefits, at least not until the age of 70. That's the way Al Gore
and the Democrats wanted it.

Because they view Social Security as a retirement program,
not welfare, Republicans have called for the elimination of the
earnings limit in every party platform since 1964 and repeal of
the earnings limit was part of the 1994 Republican "Contract
with America." While, in 1995, GOP House leaders couldn't
muster the votes to eliminate this unfair penalty for older workers, they passed an increase in the earnings limit. However, 33
Democrats blocked inclusion of the increase in the tax bill by
voting against a waiver in the rules.[124]

However, in 1996, Republicans successfully raised the earnings limit from $11,520 to $12,500 by attaching the provision to
a bill that increased the federal debt limit.[125]

By 1999, it had reached $15,500. Finally, in the year 2000, a Repub-
lican-led Congress passed legislation *abolishing the limit altogether.*

Older members of the work force were at last able to draw the full Social Security benefits they had *earned* over a lifetime.

The Clinton/Gore Administration did nothing to promote this legislation.

In *Putting People First*, their 1992 campaign tract, Bill Clinton and Al Gore promised to raise the earnings limit.[126] But they never lifted a finger to fulfill that promise, not "putting people first."

President Clinton also mentioned raising the limit in his 1999 State of the Union Address, but he never submitted legislation. The Republican House and Senate called his bluff, and he was forced to sign the bill with a frozen smile on his face.

The last time Al Gore co-sponsored legislation to raise the earnings limit was in 1977—the first year he served in Congress. After that, he backed off and never co-sponsored the measure again. But now? He takes credit for the legislation!

And what about Medicare?

In a 30-second campaign ad during the 2000 Democratic primary season, Gore depicted himself as the leader in the fight to keep Medicare solvent:

> For 70 million Americans, Medicare and Medicaid are a lifeline. Al Gore: The only Democratic candidate who saves Medicare by setting aside 15 percent of the surplus to keep Medicare solvent.

Yet Gore voted to cut Medicare as recently as 1993, when the Democrats controlled Congress.

As Vice President, he cast a tie-breaking vote for the largest tax increase in history. He didn't tell the general public that this tax bill also included *a $55.8 billion cut in Medicare benefits—and increased taxes on Social Security recipients.*[127]

And the Clinton/Gore Administration again attempted to pick the pockets of the elderly in its FY 2000 budget, which included $1.9 billion over five years in new Medicare fees for early retirees and displaced workers.[128]

Of course, both Republican and Democratic leaders knew that Medicare needed immediate attention to ensure its continued solvency. With this end in mind, a bipartisan federal commission, appointed by Clinton and headed by Sen. John Breaux (D-La.), met and formulated a proposal to reform Medicare and put it on firmer financial ground.

The plan went to the White House for approval. However, on March 17, 1999, the commission announced that the Clinton/Gore Administration had sabotaged its proposal, promising a solution of its own.[129] Breaux, a moderate Democrat, lashed out at the Clinton/Gore Administration for this rejection.

Without reform of Medicare, he said, "all you're doing is putting more money in it. But it's like putting more gas in a 1965 car. It still doesn't run any better. . . . I think what we have on the table is classic Clinton-New Democrat reform. But there are entrenched people within the White House who don't want any change."[130]

Judging from his record, one of those "entrenched people" is Al Gore.

So Gore and the Democrats continue to receive credit for supporting Social Security and Medicare when, in fact, they have sought to undermine these programs and pilfer their benefits from those they pretend to help.

On the other hand, they are now trying to dissociate themselves from another program for which liberals are totally responsible—welfare.

Welfare has been a cornerstone of the Democratic Party since the 1960s, when President Lyndon Johnson proposed his War on Poverty.

Over the next 30 years, this federal program took $5.4 trillion in tax dollars—about $54,000 for each American household today—and spent all of it on welfare. Without that expenditure, we could have avoided a national debt costing hundreds of billions in interest each year.

The results were catastrophic:

- illegitimacy increased by 500 percent,[130]
- divorce increased by 250 percent,[132]
- violent crime rose 600 percent,[133]
- and the number of families without fathers increased from 17 percent to 38 percent (up to 90 percent in inner cities).[134]

Not since Prohibition has a political initiative been so wrongheaded and so destructive. Its failures are legion—people passed out on city streets, crowded into our prisons, nursing one baby and changing diapers on two more, shooting each other in gang wars, and spaced out on drugs. All these consequences of the War on Poverty have become too obvious to hide.

So now the Democrats are running from Great Society welfare programs like rats from a sinking ship. In 1992, the year of Clinton/Gore, the party's platform called for welfare reform. Of course, neither Bill Clinton nor Al Gore had any intention of instituting genuine reform. The liberals use government handouts to buy votes. If all the welfare recipients got jobs, they would begin to bear part of the heavy tax burden on the working class— and pretty soon they'd be voting conservative. So heavy welfare rolls are in the best interest of liberal politicians like Al Gore.

Yet, with the War on Poverty tearing communities and families to pieces, these same politicians find it politically expedient to preach reform. Thus in 1994, Al Gore was saying, "We have to end welfare as we know it and emphasize the transition from welfare to work."[135]

In order to understand just how serious Gore is about reforming welfare, all you have to do is examine his voting record on the issue.

- In 1979, while Gore was still in the House, a measure was proposed that would have given eight states and three counties the freedom to reform welfare at the state and local level— and would have allowed *all* states to set work requirements for welfare recipients. Gore voted against the bill, which was defeated by a margin of only five votes. [136]
- That very same day, Gore voted to *expand* welfare and compromise states' rights. The bill, which passed, set a national minimum welfare benefit and required the *states* to provide coverage for certain families.[138]
- In 1987, while running for President, Gore dismissed criticism of the welfare system by saying, "Those people who receive welfare need it."[137] Just like that! All of them?

However, by 1992, the popular opposition to the disastrous welfare system had boiled over. Americans in growing numbers said they'd had enough and wanted welfare programs fixed or abolished. This was Leap Year, and the Democrats saw the opportunity to win back the White House after 12 years. But they needed every vote they could get from the millions on welfare.

So when reform measures came before Congress, Al Gore voted against them.

- By this time a member of the Senate, Gore voted to kill an amendment that would have allowed states to withhold welfare checks from parents of children who don't regularly attend school, thereby attempting to introduce a measure of responsibility into the system. The motion passed the Senate despite his objection.[139]

- The same year, his last in the Senate, Gore voted to kill an amendment to reduce by 10 percent welfare assistance to states that haven't instituted "workfare" programs—that is, programs designed to push welfare recipients to find jobs. (This is precisely the approach Gore now says he favors!)[140]

- Gore voted against an amendment that would have prevented welfare recipients from "shopping" for higher benefits by moving from one state to another. Specifically the bill would simply have prohibited recipients from collecting higher benefits at their new address for a period of one year.[141]

When the Republicans took over Congress in January 1995, the leadership attempted to pass two welfare reform bills.

The first of these was presented in December, along with a balanced budget package. Bill Clinton vetoed it. A few days later, Al Gore said on "Meet the Press," "We believe that welfare ought to be reformed. Now, what will the final version be coming out of Congress? We don't know. It may well be vetoed if it does not meet the standards that the President has set. But we're very much in favor of welfare reform."[142]

Less than a month later, in January of 1996, Congress sent another welfare reform bill to the White House, and the President vetoed it again.[143]

By late August of 1996, four years after the Democrats had endorsed welfare reform in their platform, the Republican Congress sent yet another bill to the White House. The President, facing the voters in the fall, finally capitulated to political necessity and signed the bill. But not after agonizing over the decision.[144] Immediately, Clinton/Gore Democrats and the press began to rewrite history *to give the President credit for this legislation*. Mindlessly pro-Clinton, *Time* magazine, in its encomium to Franklin D. Roosevelt, its Man of the Century, said of the Clinton/Gore Administration's record on welfare reform:

> One of President Bill Clinton's accomplishments has been to restore the strength of Franklin Roosevelt's legacy by reforming welfare and conquering runaway deficits while still showing how government could help average people.[145]

A lovely tribute, but untrue—and arguably an outright lie. Here's a postscript to the story:

One of the arguments Democrats used to fight welfare reform in the late 1990s was the "damaging effect" changing the system would have on children. They said children would be its chief victims, would fall deeper into despair, would be hungrier and colder and poorer than ever before.

In fact, following the enactment of the Republican Welfare Act of 1996, children actually improved economically. In 1997, as the bill was being implemented, 14.1 million people under 18 were classified as poor—i.e., 19.9 percent. By 1998, the raw number had dropped to 13.5 million, or 18.9 percent.[146]

And here's another surprise: Despite the cut in welfare, federal spending for child-related programs actually rose:

- The U.S. government provides an average of 64 percent more funding per family under the reformed welfare law than under the old one.[147]
- In 1994, the average federal subsidy per family was around $3,200 per year.[148] By 1998, it had risen to $5,300 per year.

- Funding for the Administration for Children and Families (ACF) rose from $36.6 billion in 1998 to $37.7 billion in 1999—with a request for $38.1 billion in FY 2000.[149]

In other words, when you reform a program in desperate need of reform, you don't have to sacrifice essential services. The 1996 GOP Congress understood that principle. The Clinton/Gore Administration apparently did not—or else its was playing politics with the hard-earned tax dollars of the American people and the lives of the nation's neediest and most vulnerable citizens.

Yet by the 2000 presidential primary campaign, Al Gore was *taking credit* for the legislation: "We passed tough welfare reform, which I think has worked."[150]

We passed it!

And he'll keep on taking credit for popular legislation he bitterly opposed—as long as his friends in the media let him get away with it.

7

Reinventing Society:
Al Gore on the Social Issues

By the second half of the 20th century, liberal politicians had routinely begun to flout the fundamental values that underlie American representative government and to propose radical changes—by judicial action, by bureaucratic role-making, and by executive orders.

Al Gore is at the forefront of that movement; and as President of the United States, he could institute many of those changes through *executive orders,* as Bill Clinton has already done. Anyone who believes it doesn't matter whom we elect President should keep that power in mind. When it comes to social issues, Gore has a zeal and swagger to him that Bill Clinton, even in his worst moments, lacks.

Clinton's flouting of traditional moral codes is a personal weakness. Gore's challenge to those same codes is not personal— he seems to be a good family man—but ideological. He believes in scrapping the old values as a matter of deeply-held principle.

Al Gore, like his father before him, has had to temper his radicalism in order to be elected to the U.S. Senate from the state of Tennessee. Tennesseeans have always been too conservative for the Gores, so the Gores have kept their true political agenda hidden in a lock box made of reinforced steel.

This is particularly true of abortion, one of the nation's most controversial issues. In 1992, after Bill Clinton had chosen Al Gore as his running mate, Gore announced that not only was he pro-abortion, but that "I've had the same position from the very first days in Congress."[151] And in debate with Bill Bradley, he declared that he had "always supported a woman's right to choose."[152]

No one can doubt that he's a big advocate of abortion today. In his heart, he may have been all along. But it's untrue that he has always publicly supported that view.

In 1976, a Tennessee newspaper reported Gore as saying: "I don't believe a woman's freedom to live her own life, in all cases, outweighs the fetus' right to life."[153] And that was several years after *Roe v. Wade*.

But we don't have to rely on old newspaper articles to prove that Gore once opposed abortion. We have copies of letters he wrote to constituents, making his positions quite clear—both the old position and the new one:

In a letter dated July 18, 1984, he wrote:

> As you know, I have strongly opposed federal funding of abortions. In my opinion it is wrong to spend federal funds for what is arguably the taking of a human life. I have been encouraged by recent action in the Congress, particularly in the House, that has indicated greater acceptance of our position with respect to federal funding of abortions.
>
> It is my deep personal conviction that abortion is wrong. I hope that some day we will see the current outrageously large number of abortions drop sharply.
>
> Let me assure you that I share your belief that innocent life must be protected, and I have an open mind on how to further this goal.

By 1996—when he no longer had to answer to the voters of Tennessee—he had changed his tune. In a constituent letter under the seal of the Office of Vice President, he wrote:

> I believe that personal privacy is a fundamental liberty protected by our Bill of Rights. In my view, the right to privacy includes the right to make difficult and intensely personal decisions regarding abortion. Even so, this Administration has consistently opposed late-term abortions [except] those protecting the life or health of the mother.

Even this slickly worded letter was dishonest. The Administration has never lifted a finger to prevent late-term abortions. In fact, when the Congress of the United States passed a bill outlawing partial-birth abortion—that is, killing the baby when its head was already emerging at birth—Bill Clinton vetoed it.

A second issue that has bitterly divided the nation is school prayer. Like state laws outlawing abortion, until the second half of the 20th century, no one questioned the right of schools to begin the day with a prayer. Thomas Jefferson, whose "wall of separation" phrase is frequently quoted to defend the Supreme Court's ruling, even said in his Second Inaugural Address that the states had a right to dictate religious exercises.

However, in 1962, the U.S. Supreme Court ruled prayer in schools unconstitutional—a decision that is still opposed by a vast majority of the American people.

At the beginning of the 1992 campaign, some newspapers supporting the Clinton/Gore ticket touted Gore as someone who could appeal to religious conservatives:

Thus the *Houston Chronicle* reported:

> Al Gore: A member of Congress since 1977, first in the House and since 1985 in the Senate. Gore's addition to the Clinton ticket makes it youthful, Southern and religious.
>
> Both he and Clinton are Baptists, and Gore's religious training has added a conservative mix to his politics on some issues, such as school prayer.[154]

Nothing could be further from the truth. Gore voted against measures designed to reinstitute school prayer in 1985 and 1988.

In 1985, he voted against a bill that would have barred federal courts from considering cases involving school prayer, thereby restoring a state's right to permit prayer in public schools.[155]

In 1988, Gore voted to kill the amendment to restore *voluntary* prayer in public schools by barring federal courts from hearing school prayer cases.[156]

And in the 1992 election campaign, both Gore and Clinton spoke out in opposition to prayer in schools.

And there's more.

After Gore was serving as Vice President, he took an action that defined his opposition to school prayer as nothing short of fanatic.

When it appeared that a voluntary prayer amendment proposed by Sen. Jesse Helms (R-N.C.) might have a chance to pass the Senate, Al Gore gave two anti-prayer Republican senators—John Chaffee of Rhode Island and Pete Dominici of New Mexico—a ride in Air Force II so they could be present for the crucial vote.[157]

So if Al Gore is elected in 2000, you can expect the War on Prayer to escalate.

The litmus test for liberals these days—the issue that separates the hard-core Left from the soft-core Left—is gay rights. Whatever the National Gay and Lesbian Task Force or the Human Rights Campaign demands—whether the right to serve in the military or the right to domestic partner benefits—the gut liberal must favor.

And Al Gore is the favorite candidate of gay rights activists these days. If you don't believe it, read an interview with Gore in the *Advocate* (advocate.com) entitled "Al Gore's Gay Vision." (*The Advocate* is the homosexual equivalent of *Time*.)

In introducing the interview, reporter Chris Bull writes:

> With the modern presidential campaign's mad dash for dollars, candidates maintain a furious fund-raising pace, taking a break only for rare appearances with the voters

and causes especially dear to their hearts. For Vice President Al Gore, one of those causes is gay rights. . . .

The vice president and his wife, Tipper, have boasted about the more than a dozen openly gay and lesbian aides on their staffs and count gay men and lesbians among their closest friends and confidants.[158]

If you have any doubts about the validity of Bull's comments, consider the following as proof:

- The *Washington Blade*, a homosexual newspaper based in the nation's capital, reported Gore's promise that he would establish a presidential commission to devise ways to establish domestic partnerships giving homosexual couples, as Gore put it, "the same rights as marriage."[159]
- When the Vermont Supreme Court issued a ruling saying the state had to allow homosexuals to marry or establish legally sanctioned partnerships, Gore rushed a statement to the world: "I applaud the non-discrimination and equality principles inherent in Vermont's State Supreme Court ruling this morning that same-sex couples must be given the same benefits and protections as different-sex couples."[160]
- In what was billed as "a historic meeting with national gay and lesbian leaders at his residence," Gore agreed to appoint a commission to study discrimination against homosexuals in U.S. immigration policy. Leaders of the gay rights movement complained that the new immigration bill contained no "beneficial aspects for the l/g/b/t [lesbian/gay/bisexual/transvestite] community. . . ." Their chief objection: Married heterosexual couples are encouraged in immigration policy; homosexual couples are not.[161]

- Tipper Gore, meeting with Parents and Friends of Lesbians and Gays, an activist group in Washington, told the group that a Gore Administration would "stand with you, and if necessary, fight with you."[162]

- On March 23—after the Vatican had condemned World Pride 2000, an international celebration of homosexuality to be held in Rome—Gore sent a message to the organizers of the event, wishing them success. In part he said, "As you renew your commitment to promoting equal protection under the law for every citizen and opposing all forms of discrimination, I stand ready to ensure gay and lesbian Americans have the opportunity to participate fully in a nation and a world that is united in those goals of importance to us all. I look forward to strengthening our working relationship throughout the 21st century." The Vatican protested that the event was intended as a mockery of the Jubilee Year declared by the Pope. The gay rights sponsors of World Pride 2000 saw Gore's letter as a significant victory: "This is an important message to our governments. The U.S.A., the most important in the world, and the vice president and candidate for the next election, is [sic] supporting World Pride 2000 despite all the things said and written against it."[163]

- Al Gore has pledged to overturn the ban on openly homosexual men and women serving in the U.S. Armed Forces. Leon Fuerth, Gore's National Security Advisor, speaking for the Vice President, said that the current policy—which mandates discharge if a homosexual's preferences become known—is "a posture that makes it impossible for very good people to serve without living in fear that something private about themselves will be divulged and held against them."[164]

- In early January of 2000, Gore finally said something about
  gay rights that was sufficiently outrageous to provoke back-
  lash: He said that he would require candidates for the Joint
  Chiefs of Staff to hold the belief that homosexuals should serve
  openly in the military: "I would insist before appointing any-
  body to the joint chiefs of staff that that individual support
  my policy and yes, I would make that a requirement." The
  reaction from the military and from some fellow Democrats
  was immediate. The following day, Gore said he didn't say
  it, or didn't mean, or was misunderstood, or something like
  that: "What I meant to convey was I would not tolerate, nor
  would any commander in chief, nor would any president tolerate orders not being followed."[165]

Despite these weasel words, Gore has made his position on
this subject quite clear: He will give the gay rights movement
everything it wants. And he isn't going to appoint officers to the
Joint Chiefs of Staff who hold political opinions contrary to his—
whatever the consequences to national security.

Being a liberal Democrat means you have to be fiercely,
vocally in favor of gun control laws. Any gun control laws.
Even useless control laws. After all, it's a basic assumption of
the liberal mind that all social ills can be fixed by legislation, a
Supreme Court ruling, or amending the U.S. Constitution.

In 1999, the Clinton/Gore Administration sent yet another gun
control bill to Congress; and Gore became the loudest advocate
for its passage. The Senate passed the bill, but only after a tie that
Vice President Gore himself broke. The House, however, decided
to give the bill closer scrutiny; and Gore's self-righteousness rushed
to the fore. The House leadership was dealing behind closed doors
with, among others, the National Rifle Association.

Teeth clenched, nostrils flaring, Gore told a roomful of admiring reporters: "At this very moment there are some of the other side meeting behind closed doors plotting to have more delays in order to preserve loopholes" in the bill, which would have required background checks of all firearms sales at gun shows and pawn shops.[166]

And Gore unveiled his own proposal for further gun control legislation designed to galvanize the Democratic base and thumb his nose at the Second Amendment.

Gore proposed the following new measures: (1) photo licenses for new handgun owners, (2) a ban on cheap handguns, and (3) increased spending on police training.[167]

And if that legislation were passed, he would have a new wish list to send to Congress. Yet gun control laws have never worked, and the American people know it. In fact, Gore's hardline stance on guns may hurt him with mainstream voters who just don't believe government has the capacity to take guns away from criminals.

Here's what the polls say.

- Fully 68 percent of Americans believe the best way to reduce gun violence is to enforce laws already on the books. Only a scrawny 29 percent believe the passing of new gun laws will help.[168]

- About half the people believe stricter gun legislation would have *no* effect on gun violence.[169]

- When asked why American children are violent, only 11 percent of respondents chose "access to guns." Forty-two percent said it was because parents didn't spend enough time with their children, 30 percent said it was violence on TV, 10 percent said it was a lack of good role models, and 5 percent said it was the failure of the schools to promote civility and moral values.[170]

- In the same poll, 84 percent of Americans say the best answer to gun violence in schools is greater involvement of parents in their children's lives, as opposed to only 14 percent who selected more gun control legislation. And these poll results came after a prolonged campaign by major TV networks to push for new laws restricting the purchase and use of guns.[171]

Can 68 percent of the American people be wrong when they say greater enforcement of existing laws is the answer to gun violence? Apparently the Clinton/Gore Administration believes they *are* wrong, because, while the Justice Department's budget rose by 54 percent, gun prosecutions dropped by a whopping 46 percent. Here are the figures: In 1992, under the Bush Administration, there were 7,048 prosecutions of federal firearms violations. In 1998, there were only 3,807 such prosecutions.[172]

Enforcing existing gun laws—while focusing on criminals rather than on law-abiding citizens who buy and use firearms for legitimate reasons—is clearly the answer to the problem of increased gun violence.

Given the proven record of the Clinton/Gore Administration—and Gore's own obtuse attitude—you can be certain that if Al Gore is elected President, the federal government will come after your gun, and your ability to protect yourself, and ignore the criminals who actually threaten the peace and safety of our society.

8

Captain Planet and National Defense
Commander-in Chief—Of What?

Today, with our enemies again growing in number and in strength, we have never been more open to attack.

Recently, when a Chinese official protested the presence of a Navy Task Force in the Taiwan Straits, *he reminded the U.S. government that his country possessed nuclear missiles that could reach Los Angeles.*

A small hostile nation armed with nuclear missiles could visit mass destruction on the U.S. mainland.

With our growing policy of military intervention worldwide, we need better-prepared troops, as well as new and more sophisticated weapons.

So national defense must be a major issue in the 2000 campaign.

Indeed, the President's role as commander-in-chief will be crucial in the next four years. On his performance may rest the future survival of the nation.

So what kind of commander-in-chief would Al Gore make?

We should be able to give a reasonable answer to this question by taking an unblinking look at his record on defense issues.

In August of 1996, when he was campaigning for reelection, the Vice President told a Veterans of Foreign Wars audience that he and his party were "committed to the development and deployment of even more advanced area defense theater missile defenses and were pledged to develop *by the year 2000* a national missile defense system that could be deployed as early as 2003." [emphasis added][173]

So he talks a big game when he's hanging out with the vets. But here it is 2000, and the Clinton-Gore Administration has produced no missile defense system—and there's no way that one will be in place by the year 2003.

Why?

Because both Gore and Clinton and want to spend the taxpayers' money elsewhere. Gore, who answered the call to service, as a miliary journalist behind the lines, has revealed his animosity toward the military in the votes he has cast while a member of Congress. Let's start with the missile defense system he was boasting about to the VFW crowd. No issue is more important to the safety of America today.

From the time he entered the Senate until he left it, he voted 24 times to reduce spending on missile defense systems.

- On June 4, 1985, as a freshman senator, he voted to reduce the authorization for research on this system from $2.9 to 1.9 billion—more than a third.[174] When that motion failed, he sponsored an amendment to cut the appropriation to $2.5 billion.[175] Then $2.8 billion—anything to cut funds from this program, which Ronald Reagan and the American people supported.[176]
- On August 5, 1986, he voted twice again for a reduced appropriation.[177]
- In 1988, he voted to kill an amendment to provide funds for a rapid deployment program to protect the U.S. from an accidental launch of a missile.[178] He also voted against an amendment to increase funding for a missile defense system.[179]

- In 1989, he voted against increased funds again.[180]
- In fact, his very last defense vote in the U.S. Senate was to cut $200 million from the Strategic Defense Initiative (SDI), as well as funding for the B-2 bomber, and to terminate the third Seawolf nuclear submarine.[181]

The voting record was bad enough but his reasoning was worse. On October 21, 1986, he told the *San Diego Union-Tribune* that SDI "is not viable. The Soviets have always found the rubles to match our military escalation. We're the ones with Gramm-Rudman. To assume that they're the ones who would buckle is madness."[182]

History should have set him straight. Soon—even before he left the Senate—the Soviet Empire, bankrupted financially and morally by the arms race, would implode; and the Cold War ended, not with a bang but a whimper.

You would think that Gore would have learned a lesson from Ronald Reagan: Keep the nation's defenses strong and have faith in the American free market system to outproduce the world's socialist economies and build whatever weaponry is necessary to protect the nation from its enemies.

If you want to know how much Gore learned, and how strongly he feels about national defense issues, consider the following sequence of events.

In 1991, when the question before the Senate was whether or not to support President Bush in his decision to send troops to drive Saddam Hussein out of Kuwait, Gore voted with the President. He would later say in a PBS interview:

> I was one of only a handful of senators in the Democratic Caucus in the Senate when Saddam Hussein was in

Kuwait. And the argument was made that sanctions would suffice to push him out of Kuwait and get rid of the threat that he was posing to virtually all of the Middle East. And I voted to authorize the use of force. And it felt like a lonely vote at the time. And it was tough. But I was glad that I did it. And I think, in retrospect, it definitely turned out to be the right thing.[183]

Chapter One of Volume II of *Profiles in Courage*, right?

As Paul Harvey would say, here's the rest of the story.

Up until the eve of the vote, Gore had opposed military intervention in the Middle East. In fact, on December 31, 1990, James W. Brosnan in the Memphis *Commercial Appeal* reported that "Sen. Albert Gore, Jr. (D-TN) . . . favors waiting for economic sanctions to work instead of a military strike."[184]

So what turned him around?

Bob Dole tells how Gore happened to vote against his party's position on that issue:

As late as the night before the vote, Gore was shopping around for the best deal for his vote. Gore came to me and said, "If I vote with you, how much time [to speak on the Senate floor] will you give me tomorrow morning?" This was late in the evening he came to me. Then he went to [Senate Majority Leader] Mitchell to see how much time he could get if he voted against it. . . .

He said "I'm anguishing over this. I've got to decide in the morning, and I don't know whether to vote with the President or against the President, can you give me 20 minutes of prime time?" Now, if that's commitment, it's a new kind of commitment. . . .

He was shopping. He was seeing where he could get the

most prime time on television if he voted for or against the Gulf.

He ended up voting for it. I mean that's kind of the inside joke around the Senate, the way he played it.[185]

Former Senator Alan Simpson was an eyewitness to this shameless tactic:

> That was the most troubling thing I had ever seen with any colleague ... [Gore] came to the cloakroom, and Dole and I were sitting there. We'd agreed on two hours on each side. And [Gore] said "Bob, how much time will you give me if I support the President on this vote," and [Dole] said, "How much time did they give you on the other side?" and Al said, "they said 7 minutes," And Bob said, "we'll give you 15," And then I said, "maybe we can get you another five, so you'd have 20 minutes. Al." ...
>
> The next day ... he said, "if I've got 20 minutes, I'm going to go with the President." And that's what he did. I always felt he might have had two speeches written.[186]

When he was elected Vice President, however, he became part of an Administration that was willing to sacrifice defense in order to increase give-aways and pork barrel. During its seven years of control, the Clinton/Gore Administration has cut the defense budget by 40 percent—the lowest percentage of the Gross National Product since Pearl Harbor.

Gore has even boasted about his part in crippling our Armed Forces. During an Iowa debate, he said, "I've presided over the so-called reinventing government program to downsize our federal bureaucracy, including, more than any other, the Pentagon and the Defense Department."[187]

This reckless gamble with the nation's safety would be bad enough had we kept our Armed Forces at home, engaged in training exercises, pulling KP, and occasionally helping out flood victims. But such has not been this administration's policy.

In fact, even as Clinton and Gore have reduced the defense budget by 40 percent, they have increased worldwide deployment of military forces by 2½ times. In other words, they asked America's servicemen and servicewomen to do 250 percent more work with only 60 percent of the resources.[188]

But percentages are sometimes misleading. Let's see what these figures mean in terms of personnel and equipment.

- Since the end of the Gulf War, the Army has been downsized by more than 630,000 soldiers and civilians.[189]
- Two of the ten remaining Army divisions are no longer regarded as "combat-ready" because they have fallen too far below strength.[190]
- Over 40 percent of Army helicopters are regarded as unfit to send into combat.[191]
- Over the past decade, the Air Force has been cut almost in half—from 36 fighter wings (active and reserve) to 20.[192]
- More than half of the B1-B's stationed at Ellsworth Air Force Base aren't ready for combat because there aren't enough spare parts to keep the planes in the air.[193]
- The number of ships in the Navy has been reduced from 586 to 324—and now the Clinton/Gore Administration wants to take away 19 more ships.[194]
- The average age of the B52H bombers—used exclusively in the Balkans—is 37 years.[195]
- The average age of Marine Amphibious Assault Vehicles is 26 years old. [196]

Perhaps the greatest threat to American security today is Communist China, a nation of over 1 billion people. Here is a world power that is building its nuclear arsenal as rapidly as its half-feudal, half-modern economy will allow.

Yet, as already noted, the Clinton-Gore Administration has neglected our national defense capability across the board—and in particular, it has scorned those who have repeatedly warned of the spread of ballistic missile technology.

In January of 1996, the Administration released a National Intelligence Estimate that predicted "no ballistic missile threat to the United States for at least 15 years."[197]

Many in the Clinton/Gore Administration disagreed. Thus James Woolsey, Clinton's appointee as CIA Director, told the House Committee on National Security:

> Ballistic missiles can, and in the future they increasingly will, be used by hostile states for blackmail, terror, and to drive wedges between us and our friends and allies. It is my judgment that the [Clinton/Gore] administration is not currently giving this vital problem the proper weight it deserves.[198]

In the wake of the Clinton/Gore Administration's default, the Republican leadership in Congress established a bipartisan panel, the Commission to Assess the Ballistic Missile Threat to the United States, which became known as the "Rumsfeld Commission." In July of 1998, the Commission issued its report, which brushed aside the Administration's cheery forecast in favor of harsh reality:

- The threat to the U.S. posed by these emerging capabilities is broader, more mature and evolving more rapidly than has been reported in estimates and reports by the Intelligence Community.[199]

- The warning times the U.S. can expect of new, threatening ballistic missile deployments are being reduced. Under some plausible scenarios ... the U.S. might well have little or no warning before operational deployment.[200]

Translated into everyday language, the report shows that our enemies are building missiles like crazy and that we might wake up one morning to see one dropping down our chimney.

Yet still the Clinton/Gore Administration continue to smirk at the idea there is any danger.

Then, on August 31, 1998, North Korea—small, bankrupt, bellicose, and communist—launched a ballistic missile that whistled over Japan; and, in the wake of a public outcry, the Administration had to admit its error.

Thus, in a news briefing, Secretary of Defense William Cohen said what the Administration, in the wake of mounting evidence, had been refusing to say for years: "... there is a threat, and the threat is growing, and ... we expect it will soon pose a danger not only to our troops overseas but also to Americans here at home."[201]

Then he, Bill Clinton and Al Gore stuck their heads back in the sand.

No plan to combat this new threat. No proposed legislation. The home folks—as well as our troops in the Balkans, Haiti, and elsewhere—would soon be vulnerable to missile attacks, and the Clinton/Gore Administration was preoccupied with ways to spend tax dollars on giveaway programs.

Unwilling to wait until some rogue nation mustered the nerve to lob a nuclear warhead at New York or Los Angeles, the Republican Congress passed the National Missile Defense Act of 1999—

over the objections of the Clinton/Gore Administration. The Act committed the nation to deployment of a national missile defense system as soon as the project was technologically feasible. The legislation passed the House by 345–71 (with help from 132 Democrats who smelled the coffee) and the Senate by a margin of 97–3.

As soon as the Act passed, the Clinton/Gore Administration set out to neutralize it by insisting that if we deploy a missile defense system, it must be done in conformity with the Anti-Ballistic Missile (ABM) Treaty, which gave the former USSR— *which does not exist today*—a veto over the deployment of any American missile defense system against any country in the world. At present, Russia won't give the United States its permission.

When Al Gore was asked: "Would you go forward with [a missile defense system] even if the Russians said no?" Gore replied, "Let's cross that bridge when we come to it."[202]

On second thought, let's not. Let's cross it right now—while Al Gore aspires to become Commander-in-Chief of the U.S. Armed Forces.

Epilogue

These brief chapters provide the textbook for a mini-course on an Al Gore presidency. A longer course and larger textbook would merely flesh out what we've already demonstrated—that President Albert Arnold Gore, Jr. could be an embarrassment to the American people and a threat to the stability of the nation.

To summarize, here are a few reasons why we came to this conclusion:

- His word and character are suspect. Indeed, his falsehoods and distortions rival Bill Clinton's.
- From the beginning, he's surrounded himself with people who make a profession of hustling politicians and buying favors.
- He's an ideologue rather than a thinker, a man who mindlessly supports the disastrous programs of Liberalism, unwilling to admit their failure, unable to begin the necessary search for new and better solutions to the nation's problems.
- When Ronald Reagan stood up to the Soviets, Al Gore called it "madness." Had Reagan listed to Gore there would still be a Soviet Union and a cold war. Some madness! What is madness is soliciting funds from individuals with ties to communist China or being warned about Chinese spying at our military labs and ignoring the warnings. When Gore was questioned about this, he blamed prior administrations, contrary to the truth.
- At a time when nuclear weapons are bought and sold on the international market by rogue nations, Gore has been a zealous opponent of the anti-missile system that President Reagan called for early in the 1980s.
- At a time when Americans are increasingly concerned about the moral decay of society, Gore favors scrapping the traditional values that have given shape and meaning to our civilization and substituting the loose New Age morality of the 1960s, especially with respect to America's military forces.
- Anyone who doesn't believe taxes can rise higher than they are today, hasn't listened to Al Gore or studied his voting record. Remember that Gore voted to keep higher bracket

income tax rates at 70 percent of income—so we know he'll go at least that high.

- Gore has been so unhinged by his fear of global warming and planetary destruction that he can't distinguish fantasy from reality. He's a cultist who wants the whole world to put aside its ordinary business, submit to global regimentation, and worship Gaia the earth goddess in order to save nature from people.

Over the next months, the media will attempt to camouflage much of Gore's past—his votes, his political pronouncements, his prevarications. He will be depicted as a "New Democrat," indistinguishable from "moderate Republicans," a middle-of-the-roader.

Simply by reading this book, you already know better. But you wouldn't have learned these facts simply by watching network news or reading the newspaper.

The press has been covering for Gore for decades.

We all agree that a free press is essential to the successful functioning of a representative democracy. The First Amendment to the Constitution forbids abridgment of that freedom.

But suppose we have a free press that is also dishonest—that hides facts, distorts reality, and sees the publication of news as a means of reordering society?

If the media runs true to past form, then others have to step forward and spread the truth.

That's what we've done in this book.

Now it's your turn.

Notes

1. *Los Angeles Times*, October 17, 1996.
2. *New York Times*, March 3, 2000.
3. NBC, "Meet the Press," October 1, 1996.
4. *New York Times*, March 3, 2000.
5. National Public Radio, October 10, 1996.
6. *Boston Sunday Globe*, January 12, 1997.
7. *Boston Globe*, January 15, 1997.
8. *Washington Post*, January 20, 1997.
9. NBC, "Today Show," January 24, 1997.
10. *Washington Post*, February 15, 1997.
11. U.S. District Court for the Central District of California.
12. *New York Times*, March 3, 2000.
13. Ibid., September 12, 1997.
14. White House Press Conference, March 3, 1997.
15. Associated Press, March 5, 1997.
16. *New York Times*, August 31, 1997.
17. Ibid., August 20, 1998.
18. David Johnston and Don Van Natta, *The New York Times on the Web*, March 11, 2000.
19. Ibid.
20. Speech at the Democratic National Convention, August 28, 1996.
21. CNN, "Inside Politics," March 19, 1999.
22. *Washington Post*, August 30, 1996.
23. *Newsday*, February 26, 1988.
24. *Washington Post*, February 22, 1988.
25. *Columbia Journalism Review*, January, 1993.
26. *Washington Post*, February 3, 1988.
27. *Los Angeles Times*, October 15, 1999.
28. *Newsweek*, December 6, 1999.
29. *New York Times*, November 24, 1999.
30. *Washington Post*, December 27, 1999.
31. *Buffalo News*, December 13, 1999; *U.S. News & World Report*, December 20, 1999.
32. NBC, "Meet the Press," December 19, 1999.
33. Al Gore, *Earth in the Balance*, New York: Houghton Mifflin, 1992.
34. Ibid., p. 260.
35. Ibid., pp. 325.
36. Ibid., p. 222.
37. Ibid., p. 232.
38. Ibid., p. 233.
39. Ibid., p. 275.
40. Ibid., p. 269.
41. Ibid., p. 325.
42. Ibid.
43. Ibid, pp. 325–26.
44. Ibid., 119.
45. Ibid., 308.
46. Ibid., 346.
47. Ibid.

48. Ibid., pp. 346–47.

49. Ibid., p. 347.

50. Ibid.

51. Henry I. Miller, "Gore Remakes Economics in His Own Image," *Wall Street Journal*, May 13, 1997.

52. Text of S.201, The World Environmental Policy Act of 1989.

53. Ibid.

54. Ibid.

55. Ibid.

56. *Earth in the Balance*, p. 297.

57. Ibid., p. 304.

58. Al Gore, White House Special Briefing, April 22, 1994.

59. Miller.

60. *New York Times*, November 13, 1998.

61. *Congressional Quarterly*, Vote #602, August 10, 1978.

62. Ibid., Vote #832, October 15, 1978.

63. *Congressional Quarterly Almanac*, 1981, p. 92.

64. Al Gore, 1988 Presidential Debate, February 29, 1988.

65. Ibid.

66. *Congressional Quarterly*, Vote #280, October 18, 1990.

67. "Fact Sheet on the Working Family Tax Relief Act of 1991," Bureau of National Affairs, May 6, 1991.

68. *Congressional Quarterly*, Vote #49, March 13, 1992.

69. Daniel Patrick Moynihan, *Congressional Record*, March 18, 1993.

70. "The Economic and Budget Outlook: An Update," Congressional Budget Office, September, 1993.

71. "Government Definition of 'Income' Changes, Revising Calculations of Tax Freedom Day," The Tax Foundation, April 9, 2000.

72. Associated Press, December 8, 1999.

73. *New York Times*, February 1, 1999.

74. Congressional Budget Office.

75. *Washington Post*, January 25, 1999.

76. *Sacramento Bee*, January 26, 1999.

77. Associated Press, January 26, 1999.

78. Ibid., February 18, 1999.

79. *Washington Post*, October 9, 1999.

80. U.S. Department of Education, Center for Education Statistics, *Digest of Education Statistics*, 1998.

81. William J. Bennett, *The Index of Leading Cultural Indicators*, New York: Broadway Books, 1999.

82. *Washington Post*, December 14, 1999.

83. House Republican Conference, January 5, 2000.

84. Sandra Feldman, NBC, "Meet the Press," November 7, 1999.

85. *Congressional Quarterly*, Vote #5, 1992.

86. Library of Congress, thomas.loc.gov. March 17, 1999; *Congressional Quarterly*, Vote #5, January 23, 1992.

87. *Houston Chronicle*, August 28, 1996.

88. *Milwaukee Journal Sentinel*, July 4, 1998.

89. *New York Times*, April 8, 2000.

90. United States Information Agency (USIA), Office of Inspector General, *Report of Audit*, September, 1999.

91. Ibid.
92. Associated Press, October 2, 1999.
93. Ibid., October 4, 1999.
94. *Washington Post*, October 7, 1999.
95. CBS, "Face the Nation," October 3, 1999.
96. *Time*, April 3, 2000.
97. *U.S. News & World Report*, April 3, 2000.
98. *New York Times*, April 8, 2000.
99. *Wall Street Journal*, July 10, 1998.
100. Micah Morrison, *Wall Street Journal*, September 29, 1999.
101. Ibid.
102. Douglas Frantz, *New York Times*, March 19, 2000.
103. Morrison.
104. Ibid.
105. Ibid.
106. Ibid.
107. Frantz.
108. Ibid.
109. *Washington Post*, January 26, 1978.
110. Ibid.
111. Ibid.
112. Ibid.
113. *National Review*, June 24, 1991.
114. *Newsweek*, March 23, 1998.
115. Ibid.
116. *Washington Post*, January 30, 1999.
117. *Arkansas Democrat Gazette*, February 1, 1999.
118. Editorial, *Washington Times*, August 6, 1997.
119. *U.S. News & World Report*, March 30, 1998.
120. *Washington Times*, March, 18, 1998.
121. Ibid.
122. Ibid.
123. Al Hunt, *Wall Street Journal*, March 13, 1997.
124. *Congressional Quarterly*, Vote #562, November 2, 1995.
125. *Congressional Quarterly Almanac*, 1996, pp. 2–27.
126. Bill Clinton and Al Gore, *Putting People First*, New York: Times Books, 1992, p. 141.
127. *Congressional Quarterly*, Vote #247, August 6, 1993.
128. Clinton/Gore Fiscal Budget for Fiscal Year 2000.
129. *Commercial Appeal*, March 17, 1999.
130. Paul Gigot, *Wall Street Journal*, March 15, 1999.
131. Ryan Streeter, "Welfare Reform and a More Civil Society: Fathers and Faith as Community Building Blocks," Hudson Institute, 1999.
132. Ibid.
133. Ibid.
134. Ibid.
135. *Phoenix Gazette*, April 8, 1994.
136. *Congressional Quarterly*, Vote #566, November 7, 1979.
137. Ibid., Vote #567, November 7, 1979..
138. Al Gore, 1988 Presidential Debates, November 2, 1987.
139. *Congressional Quarterly*, Vote #7, January 28, 1992.
140. Ibid., Vote #46, March 13, 1992.
141. Ibid., Vote #78, April, 10, 1992.
142. "Meet the Press," December 10, 1995.
143. *Washington Times*, January 11, 1996.

144. George Stephanopoulos, *All Too Human: A Political Education*, Boston: Little Brown, 1999.

145. *Time*, December 31, 1999.

146. *Poverty in the United States, 1998*, U.S. Census Bureau, September, 1999.

147. "Changes in Welfare Caseloads Since Enactment of New Welfare Law," Administration for Children and Families, www.acf.dhhs.gov/, August, 1999.

148. Ibid.

149. Ibid.

150. Democratic Presidential Debates, January 5, 2000.

151. *Weekly Standard*, February 14, 2000.

152. Presidential Debate, January 26, 2000.

153. *Nashville Banner*, July 29, 1976.

154. *Houston Chronicle*, July 12, 1992.

155. *Congressional Quarterly*, Vote #172, September 10, 1985.

156. Ibid., Vote #280, August 1, 1988.

157. Robert Novak, *Chicago Sun-Times*, April 21, 1994.

158. www.advocate.com

159. *Washington Blade*, February 11, 2000.

160. U.S. Newswire, December 21, 1999.

161. www.stonewalldemocrats.org

162. Associated Press, April 28, 2000.

163. CNS, April 12, 2000.

164. *Washington Times*, March 23, 2000.

165. Associated Press, January 8, 2000.

166. Ibid., May 27, 1999.

167. *Fosters Daily Democrat*, July 16, 1999.

168. "Perspectives on Gun Control," *Los Angeles Times*, March 19, 2000.

169. "Gun Control Support Muffled," ABCNews.com, April 5, 2000.

170. Frank Luntz Poll, www.yrock.com, April 6–9, 2000.

171. Ibid.

172. "Crimes Committed with Firearms," *Senate Judiciary Committee Report*, September 15, 1999.

173. Armed Forces Newswire Service, August 22, 1996.

174. *Congressional Quarterly*, Vote #100, June 4, 1985.

175. Ibid., Vote #101.

176. Ibid., Vote #102.

177. Ibid., Votes #176, #177, August 5, 1986.

178. Ibid., Vote #136, May 13, 1988.

179. Ibid., Vote #296, August 5, 1988.

180. Ibid., Vote #202, September 26, 1989.

181. Ibid., Vote #108, May 21, 1992.

182. *San Diego Union-Tribune*, October 22, 1986.

183. "Democratic Presidential Debate, University of New Hampshire," *Federal News Service*, January 5, 2000.

184. James W. Brosnan "War Fear, Recession Mean Uncertainty for New Congress," *Commercial Appeal* [Memphis], December 31, 1990.

185. CNN, "Evans and Novak," July 24, 1992.

186. CNBC, "Hardball," February 1, 2000.

187. Democratic Presidential Primary Debate, Johnston, Iowa, January 8, 2000.

188. "U.S. Military Resources Have Been Depleted by Years of Clinton/Gore Neglect," House Republican Conference Press Release, April 22, 1999.

189. Ibid.

190. Bradley Graham, "Two Army Divisions Unfit for Major War; Both Flunk Ratings of Preparedness," *Washington Post*, November 10, 1999.

191. Sean D. Naylor, "Army Aviation 'Headed in the Wrong Direction' /Composite Squadrons, More Cockpit Time Part of Planned Fixes," *Army Times*, April 17, 2000.

192. House Republican Conference.

193. Ibid.

194. Ibid.

195. Ibid.

196. Ibid.

197. Rowan Scarborough and Bill Gertz, "Missile Threat Report 'Politicized,' GOP says; Estimate Reverses Last Year's Predictions," *Washington Times*, January 30, 1996.

198. James Woolsey, Testimony before the House Committee on National Security, March 14, 1996.

199. Executive Summary of the Report of the Commission to Assess the Ballistic Missile Threat to the U.S., July 15, 1998.

200. Ibid.

201. News Briefing by Secretary of Defense William Cohen, January 21, 1999.

202. CNN, "Late Edition," April 30, 2000.